Religion and Atheism

RELIGION AND ATHEISM

by

William A. Luijpen

and

Henry J. Koren

DUQUESNE UNIVERSITY PRESS, Pittsburgh, Pa.

Editions E. Nauwelaerts, Louvain

BY THE SAME AUTHORS

Luijpen and Koren, *A First Introduction to Existential Phenomenology*, 2nd impr., 1970. 243 pages. $5.95.

Luijpen, *Existential Phenomenology*, rev. ed., 1969. 402 pages. $8.95.

Phenomenology and Metaphysics, 1965. 214 pages. $5.50.

Phenomenology of Natural Law, 1967. 249 pages. $6.95.

Koren, *Research in Philosophy*, 2nd impr., 1970. 203 pages. $4.50.

Marx and the Authentic Man, 1967. 150 pages. $3.95.

First Printing
Library of Congress catalog card number: 73-143295
Standard Book Number: 8207-0133-5
PRINTED IN THE UNITED STATES OF AMERICA

PREFACE

This book is meant to offer a relatively simple introduction to some of the problems surrounding religion and atheism. It examines the forms in which atheism presents itself today and analyzes these forms in the way they are presented by some of their most forceful protagonists. The various topics are put together under the headings of scientific, psychological, social, moral and anthropological atheism. The final chapter discusses the question of what philosophy can say about the existence of God.

At the same time attention is also paid to the many ways in which atheism manifests itself among people who affirm the existence of God. The purifying influence of atheism becomes evident in these discussions.

It is our hope that this book can be of service to many of the young people in our colleges and universities who sincerely try to reflect upon these questions.

We wish to express our thanks to Dr. James Erpenbeck for his literary revision of this work.

William A. Luijpen
Henry J. Koren

CONTENTS

INTRODUCTION

1. THE ATHEISM OF BELIEVERS AND UNBELIEVERS

Long limited to relatively restricted circles, atheism has emerged in our time as a position occupied by many people from the most diverse backgrounds. The unquestioned acceptance of God's existence that used to characterize the immense majority of men has given way in the case of many people to an attitude of questioning which often terminates in the rejection of God. The younger generation in particular, which rightly doesn't wish to accept anything merely because it is valued by their elders and institutionalized in our society, assumes a very critical standpoint with respect to the affirmation of God. There is no longer anything unusual in meeting teenagers and post-teenagers who declare themselves atheists.

"When my sixteen year old son told me that he was an atheist," a father complained, "I let him have it smack in the face." Such a striking argument for God's existence may provide an emotional release for a parent who sees one of his supreme values rejected by his offspring, but obviously can never lead to the desired goal. The young have the right to think for themselves and to reject any established value that appears meaningless to them after serious consideration. And the rejection of God is, in the eyes of many, the only position modern man can take.

It should not be forgotten, however, that atheism, as the

very term indicates, is the negation of theism, the negation of the affirmation of God. Now, it is not impossible—we should even say, it is very probable—that those who affirm God often do so in a way that cannot stand close scrutiny. Their idea of God is, at least partly, a deification of nature, of man or man-made institutions. In other words, their affirmation of God is the affirmation of an idol, a pseudo-god. In such a case, atheism, as the negation of such a god, is justified.

We do not wish to suggest, however, that every denial of God is merely a denial of pseudo-gods. There are people whose denial is directed against the authentic God. Such atheists are not necessarily insincere, lacking in intellectual acumen or psychologically disturbed. Atheism is a fundamental human possibility, for the simple reason that it is impossible for man to "see" and affirm God in the same way as he "sees" and affirms worldly reality.

If one doesn't realize that there is a difference between "seeing" and affirming God on the one hand, and "seeing" and affirming worldly realities on the other, it can easily happen that even a believer will speak about God in the wrong way, thereby reducing him to a worldly reality, a pseudo-god. As a matter of fact, this happens rather frequently; there is much atheism among believers in God, in the sense that their statements or ways of acting reduce God to an idol. That's why we spoke above of the deification of nature, man and man-made institutions.

This book, while examining the atheism of unbelievers, will also direct attention to the atheism of believers, to the tacit corruption of the affirmation of God which mars the belief of many. Still it may well be that it is not possible to totally purify the affirmation of God from all extraneous and disfiguring elements. Silence about God, one might suggest, would therefore be a better stance. Total silence, however, would mean total neglect of God and a failure to do justice to God. If we may use a comparison, language cannot adequately express genuine human love; but if love doesn't find any verbal expression at all, it runs the risk of dying. There may always be some element of atheistic distortion in our speaking about God, but there are at least certain types of atheism that can and should be eliminated from our speaking because we have come to realize that they are wrong.

Before beginning our discussion of atheism, we must pay attention to a philosopher who, in the eyes of many, stands at the beginning of the modern denial that man can affirm God's existence. This man is Immanuel Kant.

2. KANT AND THE AFFIRMATION OF GOD

In his CRITIQUE OF PURE REASON Immanuel Kant presents a detailed analysis of the traditional proofs for God's existence and comes to the conclusion that none of them succeeds in accomplishing its purpose. It would lead us too far afield to examine his analysis in detail, but his final verdict is important to us: man's theoretical reason is unable to establish God's existence. Man has no theoretical knowledge of God, and if he affirms God anyhow, his affirmation is not an act of knowledge. Kant's position seemingly—but only seemingly—justifies the conclusion that he is an agnostic, a person who holds the view that man cannot be certain about God's existence.

We said "only seemingly" because, as a matter of fact, Kant himself firmly adhered to theism. Having demolished to his own satisfaction the possibility of man's knowledge of God through theoretical reason—the reason which tells us what *is*—he re-introduces God as a postulate of practical reason in his CRITIQUE OF PRACTICAL REASON. Practical reason expresses "what ought to be." Thus it is man's ethical duties which constitute the object of practical reason. According to Kant, these ethical duties *cannot* be what they ought to be when freedom, immortality and God's existence are denied. That's why God's existence must be affirmed. But this affirmation is not "knowledge" by theoretical reason; it is a "postulate" of practical reason; his existence is admitted by an act of "rational faith."

It is sometimes claimed that Kant himself was frightened by the consequences of the conclusion he had reached in his CRITIQUE OF PURE REASON and that therefore he tried to soften these consequences by re-introducing God as a postulate of practical reason. Remove God and poor simple people would have nothing to live for, so the argument went, and out of pity for them Kant re-introduced God in his second CRITIQUE. The "real" Kant, then, would be the agnostic who denies that man can have any knowledge of God. This view, however, cannot stand close scrutiny. Kant's CRITIQUE OF PRACTICAL REASON was not an afterthought, for he planned both at the same time. And even in his first CRITIQUE he makes it clear that the agnosticism of theoretical reason can be overcome by practical reason.

But, one will say, how is it possible to deny the possibility of knowing God and, at the same time, affirm his existence? To understand this point, it is necessary to realize what knowledge meant for Kant. Living in an era in which the success of the physical sciences was evident, Kant implicitly accepted the view that knowledge, in the full sense of the term, can be attained only by the method of physical science. Now if "knowledge" means the kind of knowledge reached by physical science and we ask the question, Is it possible for man's knowledge to affirm the existence of God?, then this question means: Can physical science affirm the existence of God?

Physical science tries to understand reality by means of a quantitative approach. Within this science only that is meaningful which can be measured in some way. But a god who can be measured would be a pseudo-god, a worldly reality mistakenly called "God." Kant rightly denies that anything attainable by physical science deserves to be called "God." At the same time, however, he also rejects any claim that physical science is entitled to deny God. Physical science can neither affirm nor deny God; thus man has no "knowledge" of God.

But, according to Kant, man can affirm God's existence by an act of "rational faith." Man can and must make affirmations which go beyond the range of physical science, but these do not become "knowledge." If we keep in mind the narrow sense which the term "knowledge" has for Kant, then his admission that *rational* faith can go beyond physical science simply means that reason has also access to things beyond the reach of physical science. In other words, to drop Kant's terminology, reason, as operating in physical science, cannot reach either the affirmation or the denial of God, but reason in an enlarged sense can and, according to Kant, ought to affirm God.

If our interpretation is correct, then Kant opposed the imperialism of science, better known as scientism. He was not in any way an agnostic with respect to God's existence. One can, of course, deplore his terminology which leaves unchallenged the idea that "knowledge" is to be identified with physical science and which uses the confusing expression "rational faith" to refer to any other type of knowledge. But one who is familiar with the history of philosophy realizes how often it happens that philosophers (and scientists) fail to express their own thought correctly. For example, the terms "scientific," "objective," "subjective," "relative" and "rational" are often used in deceptive ways and therefore misunderstood.

The reason why we had to start with a consideration of Kant is the fact that Kant's proclaimed agnosticism is often held to be one of the foundation stones on which modern atheism is built. If one doesn't realize that the Kantian inability of reason to affirm God refers to reason as it operates in physical science, then Kant's critique of theoretical reason would indeed offer a strong argument for agnosticism. As a matter of fact, this point has often not been understood, thus leading to the assertion that reason, pure and simple, cannot affirm God.

After these preliminary considerations, we must now begin a study of the various forms in which atheism presents itself. They are so-called "scientific" atheism—"scientistic" would be a better term—psychological atheism, social atheism, moral atheism and anthropological atheism. Let us add at once that this division should not be understood as if these five types of atheism have nothing in common. As a matter of fact, the considerations put forward by the defenders of one form often contain elements belonging to the other forms. For instance, social atheism contains "scientific" and psychological reflections. The distinction into five main trends, then, is somewhat arbitrary; it merely refers to the most striking characteristics of the trend.

While studying these forms of atheism, we will also duly attend to the way believers in God often let their affirmation of God be influenced by faulty views; in other words, we will also study the atheistic streaks that run through many affirmations of God. This will help us to purify the question of God from elements foreign to an authentic affirmation of God. In the final chapter we will consider what, if anything, philosophy can say in reference to this affirmation of God.

SUGGESTED READINGS

Kant, *Critique of Pure Reason* and *Critique of Practical Reason.*

Luijpen, *Phenomenology and Atheism,* Duquesne University Press, 1964, Ch. I.

Ignace Lepp, *Atheism in Our Time,* Macmillan, New York, 1963.

CHAPTER ONE

"SCIENTIFIC" ATHEISM

KANT, WE SAW, resolutely rejected the idea that physical science could ever affirm or deny the existence of God. This rejection was a revolutionary attitude in an era which held science to be all-powerful and in which the scientist often felt bound to reject God in the name of science. The widespread mentality held that only that which could be verified by the methods of physical science, was real and could be affirmed as true. Let us see how this mentality came about. To do this we must begin with Galileo.

1. PHYSICAL SCIENCE AND THEOLOGY

During the Middle Ages physical science, philosophy and theology worked together in close harmony, so that one and the same man could pursue them and become, like Albert the Great, a leader in all of them. It was not merely progressive specialization that gradually drove them apart, but also a certain historical fact and the mentality which gave rise to this fact. The fact at issue was the Galileo case, in which theologians mistakenly called Galileo's scientific world-view contrary to scripture and created a situation in which he had to take an oath formally renouncing his scientific convictions about the universe.

The old world-view, which was mainly derived from Aristotle and Ptolemy, saw the earth as the center of the universe. This seemed to be demanded by "obvious" experience and confirmed by the fact that God had become man on earth. The very Incarnation made the earth the center of the universe. Celestial bodies moved around it, not driven by mechanical forces but by angels—a notion which Arabian philosophers had introduced to the West. Celestial bodies were perfect, without spot or wrinkle. The essence of everything had been fixed once and for all by the Creator; and from this essence the human intellect could deduce how things worked.

Galileo challenged this deductive world-view and appealed to experience. He held that man should examine nature and arrive at certitude about it by means of induction. Looking through his telescope, he saw spots on the "perfect" sun. The earth, he held is not the immovable center of the universe, but one of the lesser planets revolving around the sun and obeying mechanical laws.

The shock which his assertions caused was enormous. His views simply could not be true; otherwise the entire old world-view would collapse; and besides scripture itself, so it was thought, solidly supported the old view. Didn't it speak about the rising and setting of the sun and of the sun stopping in its course by divine intervention? Galileo's pertinent remark that scripture wishes to teach us how to go to heaven and not how the heavens go was simply disregarded. Both Catholic and Protestant theologians rejected his views as contrary to scripture and the Inquisition forced Galileo to renounce his views.

The implications of this condemnation were enormous. It meant that it would henceforth be impossible for a loyal Christian—or at least a Catholic Christian—to pursue physical science according to its own inherent demands: theology wished to act as a norm *within* the field of physical science. This situation officially lasted for about two centuries in the Catholic Church, for it was only in 1835 that Galileo's work was removed from the Index of Forbidden Books. Among fundamentalist Protestants it lasted even longer. As late as the 1920s a teacher was dismissed in a rural area of the United States for holding that the earth revolves around the sun.

The impetus of the new physics was not to be stopped, however. When it was not allowed to develop according to its own inherent demands within the sphere of Christian faith, it went its way outside this sphere, confident that its findings were undeniable. Belatedly the theologians realized that the new method of studying nature was not blasphemous and that its findings did not really contradict faith but merely their own hasty prejudices about nature. But by then the harm had already been done; an abyss had been created between faith and science and it proved exceedingly difficult to build a bridge.

Fuelled by the theologians' long opposition to science, a mentality had arisen which tended to reject God and religion because they were supposedly irreconcilable with science. The respectable man of science, so it seemed, had to reject God or else lead a double life: atheistic in his profession and, inconsistently, a believer in his spare time. For God did not occur among the objects attainable by physical science and God was not needed as an explanation for the findings of science. The same was true for the human soul or spirit; not a trace of it could be found under the surgeon's knife.

Much confusion about the roles of physical science, of philosophy and theology underlied such statements, but this confusion was not at all diminished by the fact that some "pious" scientists appealed to God as an explanation of physical phenomena. Sooner or later such phenomena ceased to resist scientific explanation, and each such new success of science thus appeared as yet another victory of science over belief in God.

The scientists were right, of course, in combating the theologians' opposition. But, as easily happens in a fight, the original goals were sometimes lost sight of. The legitimate desire for freedom of scientific inquiry according to the inherent demands of physical science degenerated into a kind of imperialism, a sort of absolutism: only physical science is entitled to make any meaningful statements about reality. Thus science and theology reversed their imperialistic roles. The former absolutism of theology now became the absolutism of physical science.

At one time the mentality described above was rather common. Today many reputable men of science no longer share it. But it still persists here and there. It is the mentality called "scientism." It should surprise no one that such a wide-spread, more or less unconscious attitude finally was transformed into a philosophy, a theoretical system, the system of positivism. The man who did this was Auguste Comte (1798-1857).

Comte's Positivism

Both mankind in general and each individual man in particular pass through three stages on the road to maturity of mind according to Comte. They are the theological, the metaphysical and the scientific stage.[1]

In the first or theological stage man explains everything through the intervention of gods, spirits or God. The events of nature are caused by transcendent or supernatural causes. Thunder and lightning are ascribed to a god, and so are good health, illness, fertility and barrenness. In his ignorance man simply has recourse to his imagination when he meets inexplicable phenomena. Fictitious as this religious stage is, it is nonetheless important, for it means that man has finally started to look for explanations.

In the second or metaphysical stage man no longer ascribes everything to gods, but he has learned to look for explanations within the world, immanent rather than transcendent causes. He no longer relies merely on his imagination but uses his rea-

1. Comte, *Cours de Philosophie positive,* Paris, 1830 ff., vol. 1, pp. 4 ff.

son. His reason, however, still proceeds in a very abstract way; it speaks of essences, substances, etc. as if these terms explained the way things act. But all man really does is give impressive names to the phenomena. Although the metaphysical stage is valueless as an explanation, it is important, for it means that man has given up belief in transcendent, theological explanations. Thus it prepares the way for the mind that has come of age, the mature mind of science.

In the final stage of positive science man investigates nature through experience. Giving up religious fancies and metaphysical abstractions, he limits himself to verifiable empirical laws governing the interrelationship of nature's phenomena. This is, of course, the only valid way a mature mind can proceed; and it is the way of physical science. Its method must become universal in the study of all reality. This will take some time still; in particular, there is not yet any "social physics" (Comte's term for sociology). But eventually there will be one giant system of homogeneous concepts, based on the method of physical science, so superior to everything else that theology and metaphysics will simply disappear from the scene and become topics of antiquarian interest only. God will then have vanished from the scene without leaving any unanswered questions behind. Obscurantism and backwardness will then definitely have been overcome.[2]

If Comte were to return to the earth today, about one and one half century after he formulated his positivistic philosophy, he would be sorely disappointed about the little "progress" made by the maturity of mind. Myths are appreciated today for their truth value. A scholar like Mircea Eliade[3] is world-

2. H. de Lubac, *The Drama of Atheist Humanism*, New York, 1950, pp. 127-159.

3. Mircea Eliade, *Myths, Dreams and Mysteries*, New York, 1961.

famous because of the philosophical significance he ascribes to the myths of man's most primitive religious stage. And in an era which rightly considers itself even more enlightened than Comte's own time respectable men of science, such as Friedrich Dessauer and Andrew van Melsen, can discuss the relationship between science and theology without making themselves ridiculous in the eyes of other scientists. Neither theology nor philosophy appear close to vanishing before the progress of physical science. On the contrary, many prominent men of science realize that not all the answers man needs can be given by the test tube.

Nevertheless, it remains an undeniable fact that the above-described mentality has exercised an enormous influence and that many people still adhere to it. It is the mentality of scientism, for which to know means to know as one does in physical science and to prove something means to prove it as one does in physical science. If this were indeed true, then atheism would be inevitable. This brings us to the question of physical science and the affirmation (or negation) of God's existence.

2. PHYSICAL SCIENCE AND THE EXISTENCE OF GOD

Scientism

For one who holds the view that only that is real, true or meaningful which can be verified by physical science atheism is, of course, the only possible position sound reason can hold. In one way or another, physical science verifies its assertions by measurements, a method that obviously cannot be applied to God. Thus the adherent of scientism sees himself committed to deny God's existence.

Scientism itself, however, stands on very shaky grounds. We can readily grant that *within physical science itself* only that is true which can be verified by measurements. This is simply the result of the methodic limitation which the physical scientist imposes on his study of the world. But if this principle is extended and taken to mean that in no sense whatsoever anything can be meaningful unless physical science can verify it, it becomes a contradiction, for the simple reason that in this universal sense the principle itself is not verifiable by physical science.

Secondly, scientism eliminates all ethics. From the standpoint of physical science there is no difference whatsoever between a deceased man and a murdered man, adultery and intercourse between husband and wife, surgical amputation and wanton mutilation. Yet, who will deny that there is a difference?

Thirdly, adherents of scientism usually presuppose that true knowledge is an accurate mirror image-in-the-mind of reality as it is in itself. They take for granted that mind and reality are divorced from each other—the so-called Cartesian split—and that only physical science offers accurate images of the world as it is in itself, "objectively," that is, without any additions by the mind, any limitations resulting from the attitude or standpoint of the observing subject. Today, however, prominent men of science, such as Werner Heisenberg, readily acknowledge that the answers given by science correspond to the attitude assumed by the man who questions nature; in other words, the subject's standpoint plays an important role in the answers nature gives to his questions.

Now, man can occupy many standpoints, assume many attitudes in questioning reality; the answer he gets will indicate what a particular reality is for him, the meaning it has from this or that particular standpoint. If he changes his standpoint, then the meaning of that reality will also become different. For instance, slums are not pittoresque in themselves but only from the standpoint of an artist; they are not domains of man's inhumanity to man in themselves but only for one who cares for his fellowmen. All this indicates that the meanings of the world are co-constituted by the attitudes of the subject. Only one of the many possible attitudes gives us the system of meanings known as physical science.

Differentiation of the Sciences

A science, then, corresponds to a particular attitude or standpoint assumed by man in his inquiry. He asks a particular type of question, and the result of this is that only a particular aspect of reality manifests itself to him from his standpoint. To use a comparison, nothing but light and color appear to my eyes; only the world of light and color discloses itself to my sight. Sounds are meaningless to my eyes, and colors do not appear in the world of sound open to my ears. But I am not justified in denying colors merely because I am unable to hear them.

In a similar way only various types of measurements—"meter readings" as Arthur Eddington called them—disclose themselves when one assumes the attitude of physical science. But this doesn't justify me in denying any non-measureable reality or to claim that all sciences must take over the standpoint of physical science. Borrowing a comparison of Eddington, if I go fishing with a net having a three-inch mesh, anything thinner will escape me. But this does not justify me in concluding that there are no fish thinner than three inches.

As a human being living together with my fellowmen in the world, I am "interested" in them not merely from the standpoint of "meter readings" but from many other standpoints. For example, prior to any science of psychology, I have a psychological interest in my fellowmen. Any little kid quickly learns that an argument between Daddy and Mommy is not the opportune time for asking special favors; any office boy knows that when the boss is in a bad mood, it is not the right moment to ask for a raise. The science of psychology merely takes up this original non-scientific interest and develops it in a critical and systematic way. If, swayed by the allurement of physical science, the psychologist lets himself be seduced to pursue psychology as if it were *nothing but* another type of physical science, sooner or later a crisis will arise because the psychologist notices that he is not getting where he wishes to go. If for example, he insists that puberty is nothing but a physiological phenomenon of glandular maturation, he will be unable to appreciate the adolescent's search for identity.

Accordingly, a particular science is the science it is because of the specific attitude of questioning proper to it. Only the imperialistic mentality of scientism can demand that all sciences take over the attitude of physical science. The unification of all sciences on the pattern of physical science is as utopian as the claim of the theologians who opposed Galileo in the mistaken opinion that theology can answer the questions of physical science. And the idea that if the other sciences cannot submit to the imperialism of physical science, they are meaningless nonsense is, as we saw, a self-contradiction.

Physical Science Can Neither Affirm Nor Deny God's Existence

It is hardly necessary to point out that the standpoint of physical science has shown itself fruitful beyond the wildest dreams of its earliest pursuers. The scientist wishes to question reality solely on the basis of measurements. He thereby deliberately limits himself to a specific realm in such a way that nothing non-quantitative can ever present itself to him as a scientist. His field of interest is closed to anything else. By rigidly adhering to this restriction, he has succeeded in establishing a marvellously coherent system and has penetrated deeply into the quantitative interrelationship of the objects of his interest.

At the same time, however, the standpoint of the scientist excludes from his consideration everything non-quantitative. For instance, nothing is ever grandiose, beautiful, ugly or ethical from the standpoint of physical science. If the scientist nevertheless speaks of something as beautiful or ethical, he no longer speaks as a scientist. As a human being, he obviously is able to abandon the standpoint of physical science; he is entitled to assume the attitude of a person who is interested in beauty or ethics, but when he does this he goes beyond physical science. On the basis of his science he can never affirm or deny that something is beautiful or ethical.

For the same reason the scientist can neither affirm nor deny that the objects of his inquiry are created, in the strict sense which this term has in philosophy. Creation, in the strict sense, is a concept which is utterly meaningless from the standpoint of physical science. Within the perspective open to the scientist, *as* a scientist, there is no room for anything like creation. He can neither affirm nor deny creation but can only say that his science doesn't operate with concepts like creation. This means, therefore, that the idea of a God who creates is utterly foreign to physical science, to the scientist *as* a scientist, as restricted to the standpoint of physical science.

"God is a useless hypothesis." This famous statement was the answer which the astronomer Pierre Laplace gave when Napoleon asked him what he thought of God in connection with his famous theory about the origin of the universe from a primitive nebula. From the standpoint of astronomy it is indeed one hundred per cent true that God is a useless hypothesis, i.e., astronomy never needs God as an astronomical explanation of astronomical phenomena—no more than chemistry ever needs him as a chemical factor in the explanation of chemical phenomena. But it would be wrong to misunderstand this statement as if it meant: if physical science doesn't need God to explain physical phenomena in a physical way, then God is a useless hypothesis from *every* standpoint because only physical science can ask meaningful questions. This is to claim that any question which physical science cannot answer is at most "important nonsense" because only that is true or meaningful which physical science can verify. For, as we saw, this is the self-contradictory position of scientism.

Yet it remains true that in the past—and sometimes even today—many people held the view that all true answers to all questions had to be given by one or the other of the physical sciences. Such people simply were victims of scientism. Not all of them, however, denied God; some believed in him and tried to prove his existence by means of physical science.

"Scientific" Proofs for God's Existence

Physical science in its modern form originated in the seventeenth century, but for a long time no one knew exactly what physical science was. The new science was so busily engaged in pursuing its exciting line of research that there was scarcely any time and interest to reflect on what exactly the scientist was doing. It was thought that physical science was merely a new kind of philosophy; as a matter of fact, the title of Isaac Newton's main work was MATHEMATICAL PRINCIPLES OF NATURAL PHILOSOPHY. And to this very day in the English-speaking world the successful graduate student in any of the physical sciences gets a doctorate in *philosophy*. The distinction between philosophy and physical science was not yet clear.

This situation accounts for the fact that "pious" scientists tried to counteract the atheism to which physical science was supposed to lead by offering "scientific" proofs for God's existence. One of the best-known attempts is that of Rudolf Clausius (1822-1888), a German mathematical physicist, famous for the introduction of the concept of entropy, who derived a proof for God's existence from this physical concept. Other well-known attempts are the biological proofs of the French-American Alexis Carrel (1873-1944) and Lecomte de Noüy. We will not examine such proofs in detail but limit ourselves to the following remarks.

From the preceding considerations it should be evident that such kinds of proof must fail; they try the impossible by going beyond the range to which physical science limits itself. Physical science wishes to concern itself only with material reality subject to measurement, to measurable factors immanent in the world. Hence the reality of something transcending the world, a transcendent God, simply lies beyond its reach.

While studying the material world, physical science meets riddles, enigmas which it is not yet able to solve. When this happens, there is always a temptation to "illuminate" such a dark corner by saying that God himself is at work there, that the puzzling phenomenon is caused by God. This is a very old temptation. When people didn't understand thunder and lightning, they ascribed them to Zeus or some other god. But today this dark corner no longer needs God as an explanation. A similar fate has befallen the various gods of the sun and the moon, gods of harvest and hunt, and fertility gods. Any kind of god who hides in a dark corner of the world not yet illuminated by physical science will sooner or later be expelled and unmasked as a fake, a pseudo-god.

This is as it should be. The riddles encountered by physical science in its own field are riddles to be solved by physical factors, worldly realities, and not by a supra-worldly or transcendent God. And any "pious" scientist who appeals to God as the physical explanation of a particular physical phenomenon encountered in his physical research fails to recognize God's transcendence of the world. He reduces God to an object within the world, to a physical cause. Thus he denies the transcendent God and professes a kind of atheism.

The riddles encountered by physical science are not "open doors" leading to God, but merely invitations to the scientist to pursue his inquiry and find a physical factor as a physical answer to his physical question. It is true, of course, that any such answer raises further questions demanding new answers, but as long as man holds fast to the line of research pursued by physical science, as long as he assumes the standpoint of physical science, he can, in principle, never reach a non-measurable reality. Let us keep in mind, however, that physical science is only one of the many possible standpoints or attitudes of man. Not all reality discloses itself to man when he occupies this particular standpoint.

Metaphysics concerns itself with the problem of God's existence. But metaphysics should not be conceived as if it were a continuation of physics. Matters should not be presented as if when the physicist is stuck for an answer to a physical problem, the metaphysician, untrained in physical science, can continue *the same line* of questioning and come to the rescue of the physicist. The scientist and the metaphysician may occasionally use the same terms, but these terms do not have the same meaning.

For example, the astronomer studies the origin of the universe, but his astronomical problem as such doesn't interest the metaphysician when he ascribes the origin of the universe to God. The metaphysician who affirms that the universe owes its existence to an act of creation by God bases himself, as we will see, on the contingency of the world, on the consideration that the beings of the universe do not have within themselves a sufficient reason for their existence. But he is not particularly interested in the question whether the universe has always existed or came to be "in time," for this question has no bearing on his problem. As a metaphysician, he is even less interested in the kind of condition the universe was in if and when it came to be and the various stages of its development. Differently expressed, the horizontal lines of interconnection between the beings of the universe are not his concern; what he considers is the vertical line of dependence on a transcendent cause which all beings of the universe, he holds, have at every moment of their existence.

This line of thought is utterly foreign to any kind of physical science, regardless of its stage of development. Newtonian physics is neither closer nor farther away from it than is Einsteinian physics; neither has anything to do with it. In no stage of development does any physical science ever demand an appeal to God as the explanatory hypothesis of its own problems. And for the same reason physical science can never demand the denial of God.

Short-sighted scientism, we may say, moved some scientists in the past to deny God's existence. But it would be just as short-sighted to say that today science is moving closer to affirming the existence of God. At most one can say that the modern theories of science tend to make scientists more cautious and less absolute in their claims. They thereby tend to create a psychological climate in which it is more difficult for the *man* who is a scientist to reject God on the alleged basis of his scientific knowledge.

3. THE PROGRESS OF SCIENCE AND THE ABSENCE OF GOD

In former times, so it is often said, man could see God everywhere in his world. Having hardly any power at all over nature, man was simply forced to abandon all responsibility for it to God. Good health as well as sickness, an abundant harvest as well as drought, disasters and good fortune—all came from the hands of divine Providence.

But today, again it is often said, the situation is different. Man has come of age and is his own master. Physical science and technology have given man much control over nature. Good health is the result of a highly developed science of medicine and medical services. If an epidemic breaks out, it is no longer an "act of God"—except as a standard expression used by lawyers—but something for which we blame the responsible public health officials. If a building is struck by lightning, we no longer see it as a divine punishment, but as an electrical phenomenon that could have been avoided by the installation of lightning rods. And an abundant harvest is viewed as a triumph of scientific fertilizers and pesticides, not as the result of praying on rogation days. Man, so it is often said, no longer needs God; he can take care of himself. Small wonder, then, that God is absent from the world as never before. The more science progresses, the less room there seems to be for God.[4] God has become a Displaced Person.

A faulty idea of God underlies this picture, in which man's development of technology is seen to lead to the disappearance of God. We find this idea already clearly expressed in the old Prometheus myth. Prometheus was a hero who stole fire from heaven. Given the choice of returning it to the control of the gods or to be forever chained to a rock, Prometheus replied: "I'd rather remain chained than become again a slave of Zeus." Fire gives man the power to transform ore into metal; it mysteriously enables man to take care of his needs. (In ancient myths and sagas the blacksmith often plays an important role). By stealing fire from the gods, Prometheus made man less dependent on the gods, who jealously wished to keep man in bondage. God and man, then, are seen as competitors in this myth.

If man had indeed to choose between slavery to the gods or God and self-determination through the development of his potential, he should, of course, side with Prometheus. But Zeus is not the transcendent God of Judeo-Christian revelation but a pseudo-god. The transcendent God doesn't object to man's self-development. On the contrary, he explicitly gave man the mandate to subdue the earth and make it subservient to himself. Scientific progress and technological development, then,

4. Albert Dondeyne, *Faith and the World*, pp. 109-125.

do not remove God from the world; atheism is not necessarily a concommitant of man's progress.

It must be admitted, however, that very often believers in God failed to recognize his transcendence and considered technological progress an interference with God's designs. They thereby placed man and God in competition. This happened in particular when God was seen as a God of nature. Such theists objected, for example, to the introduction of lightning rods: God wishes to strike the wicked with a bolt of lightning, but, lo and behold, the wicked puts up a metal rod and frustrates "God's will." Incubators also were against God's will, for he had ordained that eggs should be hatched by hens.

Similar arguments were—and sometimes still are—used against inoculation, blood transfusion, painless childbirth, etc. One could argue in this way against smoking. "If God had wished man to smoke," said a minister of a non-smoking sect to his physician, "he would have put a smoke-stack through man's head." "Is that so?," the doctor parried, "in that case I had better not operate on your gall bladder. If God had wanted me to operate on you, he would have put a zipper on your stomach." To give another and more serious example, when in 1969 Hurricane Camille struck Mississippi, causing many death and enormous damage, a clergyman preached the following Sunday that "God had wanted to show man who is boss."

But what kind of a god is that who feels the need to show man who is "boss" by going on a rampage and killing scores of people? If he were a man, he would be executed for mass-murder or at least given a life sentence because of his failure to live up even to the minimum of respect man is entitled to. The idea underlying such a concept of God is that man's self-sufficiency through science and technology is somehow wrong and that, therefore, from time to time man needs to be put in his place. Besides, God is identified with nature or at least his causality is reduced to a physical factor operating in the universe, a factor which man could counteract through his ingenuity, but only under pain of going against "God's will."

In the eyes of modern man there is no longer room for such a god, and rightly so. But, as we saw, this kind of god is not the transcendent God of Judeo-Christian revelation. The denial of such a pseudo-god is a good kind of atheism. One could object and say that man is still far from self-sufficient and that there will always remain worldly needs which only God can fill. For example, man can do very little to control the weather, to heal incurable diseases, to avoid wars, etc. Thus he remains dependent on God; God remains present to him as a reality in such matters and that's why man continues to pray to God.

Such an objection again takes refuge in a dark corner not yet illuminated by science. What man cannot do today, he will sooner or later be able to accomplish. A god hiding in such a dark corner would again be chased away and replaced by man. There simply is no worldly need with respect to which one can confidently say that it lies beyond man's potential ever to fill it. Besides, by claiming that, e.g., the avoidance of war is beyond man's power, one invites people to resign themselves to their fate and offers them an alibi for not doing anything to banish war: man is not guilty because it is beyond his power.

God, it is often said, was invoked more frequently in the past than he is today. The whole of life in more primitive times seemed permeated with religious practices. Helpless as he was, man turned to God for everything. But today he is no longer as helpless and therefore he invokes God less or even not at all. This idea can be popularly expressed by saying that religion began to decrease when man invented artificial fertilizers. The big question, however, is whether the alleged religiousness of former times was authentic religiousness or a camouflaged form of atheism, a denial of the transcendent God, pseudo-religion masquerading as religion.

A farmer who stops praying for an abundant harvest because he now has chemical fertilizers and scientifically selected seed merely views God as an agricultural factor; for one who gives up prayer because modern medicine can help him, God is merely a super-physician; one who no longer prays because he can get psychiatric help views God as a super-psychiatrist. In all such cases God is simply reduced to a causal factor within the world. The progress of science has indeed eliminated the need for such a pseudo-god. Today it is no longer easy to present a pseudo-god as if he were the transcendent God.

For the believer in the transcendent God, God is no more or no less present in the world of the primitive man than in our modern world, but his presence is not like that of a worldly cause. He is present in it as the transcendent Creator; his presence is an "absent presence," that is to say, he is not present among the worldly factors operating in the universe, he cannot be manipulated by prayer just as worldly factors are manipulated.

To finish this chapter, let us add that in the preceding paragraphs we have only considered man's worldly needs, with respect to which God does not operate like a worldly factor. We did not at all imply that man's needs are fully circumscribed by the world, that he lacks transcendent needs, that he is nothing but a project of the world. We did not even imply that all recourse to God with respect to worldly needs is below the dignity of man now that he has come of age or that such prayers are meaningless. We cannot develop this point fully here because it would have to be based on theological considerations and thus lies outside the scope of this book.

One remark, however, can be made. It is that authentic prayer is not an attempt to manipulate God but a loving relationship to a God who invites us to call him "Father." To use a comparison, a woman who cleverly coddles and humors her husband with an external display of love in order to get what she wants manipulates her husband; somewhat in a similar way pseudo-prayer tries to manipulate God. But a woman who authentically loves her husband can still ask him what she wishes without any attempt to manipulate him. She is certain in her knowledge that the beloved will do whatever he can out of love for her, and she doesn't consider asking below her dignity because her relationship is one of love. In a similar fashion it is not against man's dignity for the authentic believer to ask his loving Father for whatever he needs; at the same time he is certain that the God of love will grant him whatever authentic love is able to grant.

SUGGESTED READINGS

Auguste Comte, *The Fundamental Principles of the Positive Philosophy*, tr. by P. Discours and H. Jones. Contains only the first two chapters of Comte's six volume *Cours de Philosophie positive.*

Luijpen, *Phenomenology and Atheism*, Chapter Two.

Joseph J. Kockelmans, *Phenomenology and Physical Science*, Duquesne University Press, 1966.

Albert Dondeyne, *Faith and the World*, 2nd impr., Duquesne University Press, 1965, Ch. IV.

CHAPTER TWO

PSYCHOLOGICAL ATHEISM

1. INTRODUCTION

How is it possible, many atheists ask themselves, that people who in other respects are intelligent, even prominent in some field of human endeavor, continue to affirm the existence of God? One does not need to affirm the reality of God to excel in any of the physical, human and cultural sciences or mathematics; why, then, do intelligent people persist in believing in him?

As we saw in the preceding chapter, it is not science but scientism that makes the affirmation of God impossible. One who rejects the absolutism of science can still affirm God's existence. But scientism presents itself in many forms. One of these we have discussed in the preceding chapter, viz., the absolutism of physical science. In the present chapter we will discuss a form of psychological absolutism, so-called psychologism.

The atheist is convinced that God doesn't exist, but he cannot disregard the fact that many intelligent people continue to affirm him. To explain this fact, he then has recourse to a psychological explanation: people who affirm God suffer from some kind of mental aberration. There are all kinds of psychological explanations for the belief in God, but their common element lies in so-called "projection."

The term "projection" was first used in its psychological sense in connection with problems about the reality of colors and visual perception of space. In this sense projection theories can be found in Locke, Berkeley and Kepler. In a broader sense one may speak of projection whenever people ascribe their own qualities to others; they look at others through the "spectacles" of their own dispositions. For example, one who likes to cheat people will be inclined to suspect others of being cheats. As used in this chapter, however, the term "projection" will refer to the theory that man detaches the best of his own being from himself, construing it as a higher or highest being outside himself. He then bows down before it as if it were an independent and alien being, without realizing that he is "really" bowing down before himself.

The best known and classical example of a religious theory of projection is that of Sigmund Freud. We will consider it here.

2. THE PROJECTION THEORY OF FREUD

Freud's main discussion of religion is found in THE FUTURE OF AN ILLUSION, TOTEM AND TABOO and MOSES AND MONOTHEISM. In the first of these, he argues that religion is nothing but a scheme by which man tries to defend himself against the overpowering forces of nature. He begins by humanizing these forces, that is, he presents them as if they were human beings. In human society people can be pleaded with, they can be bribed and pacified. By being humanized, then, the forces of nature lose their fearful character at least to some extent. Man can then practice with respect to them what he also did as a child in reference to his father. The child's attitude to his father is always ambiguous; the father is both loved and feared, he is the one who is expected to protect his son but, at the same time, he is also feared, for he can also hurt his son. Man, says Freud, ascribes the same fatherly attitude to the forces of nature; and when he makes gods out of nature's forces, he assumes in their respect the same ambivalent attitude as he had toward his father.[1]

In a subsequent stage of development man discovers the laws which govern nature, so that the forces of nature lose their human characteristics. But man continues to feel powerless in reference to nature. That's why he now ascribes to the gods the function of making up for the deficiencies of his own cultural development. The gods must alleviate man's suffering and guard the morality demanded by culture. A rich and variegated religious imagery results from man's helplessness, but it all contains the common implicit element of the father image. When man finally realizes that this common element underlies all these images, he merges them into a single image of one God, his Father. Now his childlike attitude toward God can grow further and attain its full development.[2]

In TOTEM AND TABOO Freud tries to burrow even deeper into the father image buried in every image of God. Totemism, he says, was the first religion of man. Now, the totemistic meal plays a crucial role in totemistic religion. In preparation for this meal, all members of a tribe catch the totem animal and savagely kill it by beating it to death or tearing it to pieces alive. Then they devour the meat raw. In ordinary circumstances no one is allowed to kill a totem animal, but the tribesmen feel that doing it all together is justified. Once the deed is done, they mourn the dead animal, trying as it were, to cleanse themselves of responsibility for its death. Wild festivities follow the mourning ritual.[3]

Freud's interpretation of all this is as follows. The totem ani-

---

1. *The Future of an Illusion*, pp. 28 ff.
2. *Ibid.*, pp. 30 f.
3. *Totem and Taboo*, in *The Basic Writings of Sigmund Freud*, pp. 914 f.

mal stands for the father. Man's feelings toward the father are always ambiguous, a mixture of love and hatred. That's why mourning as well as joy surround the death of the father symbol. More light is thrown on this entire question, Freud says, if we join this psychoanalysis with the Darwinian hypothesis of the primitive horde.[4]

In the primitive horde a jealous father kept all the females for himself, thereby frustrating the sexual cravings of his adolescent sons. Finally the brothers joined forces, killing the father and then devouring him. Together they dare to do what none of them alone could accomplish. By eating their father, they identified themselves with him and acquired his power. The totem meal, says Freud, is a symbolic repetition of the original deed and, at the same time, the beginning of social organization, moral rules and religion. He explains this as follows.

The brothers' hatred of their father vanishes after they have murdered him, but their love of the father remains. That's why they are sorry for what they have done. To atone for the murder, they prohibit the killing of the totem animal (the father's symbol), they renounce relations with the father's females by proclaiming the prohibition of incest and imposing the law of exogamy. These two fundamental taboos (killing the totem animal and incest) correspond to the two aspects of the Oedipus-complex with which morality began. Moreover, after the father's death, the brothers became competitors for females; to preserve their social organization, they had to prohibit incest.

The beginning of religion manifests itself in the other taboo. The prohibition against killing the totem animal is like a contract with the father: the sons bind themselves to spare his life, and the father binds himself to give his sons protection. All religions, says Freud, attempt to solve the problem of guilt arising from the murder of the archfather. At this stage of our inquiry, then, Freud argues, we can draw these conclusions:

4. *Ibid.*, p. 915.

1. Society is based on complicity in a common crime;
2. Religion is based on the sense of guilt and remorse;
3. Morality is based on both social necessity and the expiation demanded by man's sense of guilt.[5]

Deification of the Father Image. In the next stage of its development religion makes the ancient totemistic meal reappear in the form of a primitive sacrifice. But there is a new element here, viz., the presence of the tribal god. But god, as we saw, is nothing but a sublimated father-image. This, therefore, means that the father is twice present in the primitive sacrifice: first, as the sacrificial totem animal and then, as the god to whom the animal is offered. How can this be?

Freud argues that the totem animal was the first father-surrogate and that later a second father-surrogate was added because in the course of time man's attitude toward the father underwent a change. The murder of the archfather created a powerful longing for the father; yet none of the murdering sons could equal the father and thus fill their longing. Forgetting the bitterness which originally had led them to kill the father, the sons' longing increased and gave rise to the father ideal. They deified their murdered archfather, thus raising him far above their own level. At the same time, their society could now develop into a patriarchal system: there could be fathers again, but they would have only limited powers, so that they would never approach the position of the archfather. In this way the unsatisfied longings for the original father could continue; in other words, religious longings will continue to exist.[6]

Further Development of Religion. Subsequently, the totem

5. *Ibid.*, pp. 916 ff.
6. *Ibid.*, pp. 919 ff.

animal began to lose its sacred character; the sacrifice also lost its connection with the totemistic feast and became the simple offering of gifts to the deity. God is now so high above all things human that he can be approached only through priests as consecrated intermediaries. Yet even now there remain anti-father sentiments. This is evident from the fact that ancient Semitic religions demanded a yearly sacrifice of a god; and elsewhere human beings were sacrificed as representatives of the gods.

At the same time, the son's ambiguous attitude toward the father makes him try to put himself in the place of the father-god. This is particularly evident in Christian religion. So-called original sin is an offense against God the Father, and Christ redeemed mankind from this sin by the sacrifice of his life. By sacrificing his life, Christ effected the reconciliation of mankind with the Father, but the anti-father sentiments also triumphed: the son himself becomes a god, and the religion of the Father becomes a religion of the Son. A sign of this substitution is that the ancient totem meal is revived in Christianity in the form of communion. The brothers no longer eat the flesh and drink the blood of the Father but that of the Son. They wish to identify themselves with the Son and reject the Father. Thus Christian communion is nothing but a repetition of the ancient crime of revolt against the father.[7]

In MOSES AND MONOTHEISM Freud presents an even more detailed picture of the development of religion toward the monotheistic forms of Jewish and Christian religion. We may omit this here, for what we have seen above suffices to show Freud's approach to religion. We must add, however, a few other remarks about the objective value of religious ideas which Freud presents in THE FUTURE OF AN ILLUSION.

7. *Ibid.*, pp. 922 ff.

Religion as an Illusion

If one critically examines religious ideas, says Freud, one discovers that they are nothing but illusions, the illusory fulfillment of "the oldest, strangest and most insistent wishes of mankind." Feeling helpless, a child craves protection, and this protection is given by its father. But this feeling of helplessness persists throughout life and thus gives rise to the illusion of an all-powerful Father-God. The idea of the Father-God is an illusion because it is based on a wish-fulfillment and disregard for reality: "It would be very nice if there were a God who created the world and was a benevolent Providence, and if there were a moral order in the universe and an afterlife; but it is a very striking fact that all this is exactly as we are bound to wish it to be." People uncritically assume the reality of God because they always tend to be naive in religious matters. But there is, of course, only one way by which objectivity can be reached, and that is the way of science. It is an illusion to assume that what science cannot give us we can get elsewhere.[8]

As an illusion, religion should be unmasked. But, Freud asks himself, would that really be such a good idea since virtually everything of value in our culture is based on religion? Wouldn't the world return to chaos if we unmasked religion? Freud's answer to this self-made objection is that he is not doing anything new by exposing religion; he has merely provided a psychological foundation for it. Moreover, believers will simply disregard what he says anyway because they are firmly established in their faith and unmoved by psychological explanations: "It is painful to think that the great majority of mortals will never be able to rise above this view of life." Finally, the unmasking of religion may be disastrous at first

---

8. *The Future of an Illusion,* pp. 52 ff.

blush, but in the long run the preservation of religion will be more harmful than its exposure.[9]

Great as the contributions are which religion has made to culture, in particular by establishing controls over unsocial passions, it has not done enough, says Freud. It has failed to give happiness to most people, for they continue to view the control over their passions as an undesirable yoke and threaten to throw it off. Chaos can result, of course, when man realizes that religion is an illusion. This discovery, however, is unavoidable, for with the progress of science their faith will be undermined. But the threatening chaos can be avoided if culture and morality can be anchored in reason and science instead of religion. This substitution of reason for religion would in fact provide a better foundation for morality. For religion absolutizes its moral rules, making them impossible to change. As long as religion sanctions morality, then, no progress can be made. Thus the rejection of religion is the promotion of culture and morality.[10]

The objection could be raised that Freud is inconsistent. He first bases morality on the irrational foundation of the totemistic taboo and now pleads for a rational foundation of morality. Freud's answer is that there is no inconsistency. Like the individual child, mankind as a whole, in its growth to maturity, passes through periods that resemble neuroses. A child had its period of neurosis because the passions are too strong to be handled rationally and have to be repressed. But such a neurosis is either spontaneously overcome in the process of growing up or can be cured by psychological treatment. The same happens to mankind as a whole: as long as the passions cannot be handled rationally, they have to be repressed, and this gives rise to the collective neurosis known as religion. As a matter of fact, Freud adds, strongly religious people seldom suffer from

9. *Ibid.*, pp. 62 ff.

10. *Ibid.*, pp. 66 ff.

a personal neurosis; having deeply plunged into their collective neurosis, they need not nourish a personal one. But just as in the normal process of growing up the childhood neurosis is spontaneously overcome, so mankind will normally overcome its collective neurosis when it becomes more mature. We are now, says Freud, in the period of transition to the condition where mankind will be free from the collective neurosis of religion.[11]

3. CRITICAL REFLECTIONS

It is not our task to examine the psychology of religion presented by Freud; only psychologists can be competent in such matters. Undoubtedly it is true that Freud has made psychological observations about religion that are of importance for the believer's reflection upon God and religion. This is, for example, the case when he speaks of transference: "The personal attitude of man toward God depends on his attitude toward his human father and . . . it changes and evolves accordingly."[12]

Moreover, Freud offers a view of man in dynamic terms, with specific descriptions of psychic dynamisms. And he did this at a time when man's concepts in many fields were assuming a dynamic dimension. For physical science the cosmos is not a static system but a dynamic interplay of forces, with respect to which man is not a "disinterested spectator" but an active participant, who himself has arisen through a dynamic process of evolution. Society, as Marx showed, is not a static entity confined within very restricted limits but a complex whole in which all kinds of subtle "forces" are dynamically at work and lead it forward to new stages which man himself must control. Freud offers us a view which extends this dynamism to man's own psyche. This raises a stimulating problem of great interest

11. *Ibid.*, pp. 75 f.
12. *Totem and Taboo*, pp. 919.

for religion: Is there any specifically religious dynamism? And if so, how does it work? How does it relate to other psychic dynamisms?

Finally, man's idea of himself greatly affects his idea of God. In the Judeo-Christian tradition man views himself as "God's image and likeness." Thus it stands to reason that his concept of God will be influenced by his self-understanding. In this sense all theology is, as Feuerbach expressed it, anthropology (cf. Ch. III). If man has a dynamic concept of himself and his world, then the religious man will view himself as an image and likeness of a *creative* rather than just an *intelligent* God. The accent will fall then on action rather than contemplation, on love and its creativity in human relations rather than preservation of the established order. God will then be for man a challenge and an invitation to go forward rather than a command to stay in his appointed place. And the better he understands the driving forces that are at work in the human substructure, the better also will he be able to make them subservient to his dynamic self-understanding in terms of his self-project and the project of his co-existence with his fellowmen.

Freud also deserves credit for drawing attention to the connection that often exists between religion and inhibition. "Guilt feelings" can be infantile regressions, resulting from the failure to observe taboos which are mistakenly confused with authentic moral norms and are enhanced with an aura of sacredness by a distorted sense of religion. But irrational taboos have nothing to do with authentic religion. Authentic moral norms, as we will see in connection with Nietzsche, arise from man's personal understanding of what is demanded by the fact that he is a human being and has to realize himself as such together with his fellowmen in the world. The "guilt feelings" which arise in an individual when he becomes conscious of falling short of an authentic moral demand—in Christian terms, "sin"-

consciousness—should not be confused with the "guilt feelings" originating in the violation of a taboo. An authentic moral demand is never a taboo.

It is true, of course, that many people don't distinguish between these two types of guilt feelings because they have not reached the level of an authentic moral consciousness. In connection with this it may be useful to point out that Freud, by his own admission, never observed any genuine religious experience either in himself or in anyone else. But this is a very shaky foundation for conclusions about religion as such, especially if one considers the way religion was often understood by ordinary people in the era of legalistic morality in which Freud lived. Yet Freud's analysis has contributed to our greater consciousness of the distinction between authentic morality and religiousness on the one hand, and taboos and pseudo-religiousness on the other.

Let it be noted in passing that anthropologists also criticize Freud's TOTEM AND TABOO as a fanciful reconstruction presenting itself in the guise of a scientific analysis. And they draw attention to its inconsistencies; for example, the primitive horde is supposed to be subhuman, yet Freud ascribes to it human characteristics, such as guilt feelings, which are unknown below the human level.

Our main concern is the philosophical aspects contained in Freud's theory. First of all, it should be noted that one doesn't have recourse to a theory of projection unless one "sees" nothing where others "see" something. This means at once that a projection theory of religion must start from the premise that God doesn't exist and then, on the basis of this premise, develop an explanation as to why some people continue to affirm God. The psychologist who offers an explanation of religious phenomena may tell us many useful and interesting things, but a philosopher must ask himself what remains of the psychologist's claim that religion is *nothing but* a projection *if God really exists.* For psychology as psychology can never prove that there is no God; psychology can explain psychical phenomena, but it can never establish that God is nothing but a psychical phenomenon.

If a psychologist nonetheless makes such a claim, then he is indulging in psychological scientism or psychologism. He then asserts that only psychology can decide whether anything real corresponds to the ideas in man's mind and that, once psychology has spoken, there is nothing more to be said. In other words, he presents his view as a theory of reality which is, in principle, "complete": only that exists or is real which psychology can verify. This is the same kind of imperialism which used to characterize physical science in the past and which is, as we saw, a *philosophical* theory containing an implicit contradiction.

Freud indulged in this kind of scientism. It made him neglect to devote any serious consideration to the question of God's existence. For him it is *a priori* certain that a negative answer must be given to this question, for "scientific work is the only road which can lead us to a knowledge of reality outside ourselves."[13] If science cannot say anything about God, says Freud, religions speaks about something that is beyond scientific critique; therefore, no one will any longer be interested in God. This is scientism pure and simple.

Secondly, belief in a provident God and an afterlife obviously are "wish-fulfillments," says Freud. We wholeheartedly agree, of course. But does it follow that *therefore* they obviously are not objective? Is everything that corresponds to a deep-felt wish *per se* not objective, not real? The fondest wish of a lover is that his beloved reciprocate his love; may we

13. *The Future of an Illusion*, p. 55.

say that *therefore* she does not love him? Some wish-fulfillments obviously are mere wishes; others are not. The mere fact that something is a wish-fulfillment does not automatically exclude its objective reality. Whether a particular wish-fulfillment is real or not cannot be decided on the basis of its psychological condition of corresponding to a wish, but must be settled by an investigation on the appropriate level; with respect to God this level is that of philosophy and not that of psychology. And on the philosophical level one cannot settle the matter by *a priori* identifying all reality with material reality.

When psychology degenerates into psychologism, it must expect that it will be attacked with the very weapons it has forged. When one psychologist uses psychoanalysis to reduce the religion of another to an Oedipus-complex which has not been eliminated in time, he should expect that another psychologist will use psychoanalysis to unmask his colleague's atheism. As a matter of fact, this has happened. Analyzing Freud's antireligious attitude, Gregory Zilboorg[14] came to the conclusion that it could be traced to Freud's pessimism which itself resulted from the affective frustration he suffered when he was three years old. It stands to reason that now a third psychologist can try to explain Zilboorg's psychological analysis of Freud's atheism by psychoanalyzing Zilboorg. And so on *ad infinitum.* All this, however, does not tell us anything whatsoever about atheism and theism as such. This question can only be answered by going beyond the standpoint or attitude assumed by the psychologist as such. Philosophical questions can neither be answered by psychology nor reduced to psychological questions.

To use a comparison, once upon a time there were two brilliant physicists who detested each other. Whenever the one put forward a new argument in favor of a particular theory, the

14. *Freud and Religion,* Westminster, 1958.

other felt psychologically compelled to contradict him at once by writing an article against his view. The psychological explanation of their positions is very easy, but it doesn't bring us one step closer to deciding which of the two is right. That can be decided only by examining the validity of the physical arguments which, in their mutual animosity, they bring to bear against each other.

The same is true of Freud's position with respect to religion. Only an examination of the philosophical arguments he brings to bear against the reality of God and the authenticity of man's religious dimension can be decisive. But, as we saw, such arguments are conspicuously lacking; the whole matter of God's existence is *a priori* settled for Freud. And with respect to religion, he simply proceeds on the basis of things which today we would consider pseudo-religiousness rather than authentic religion.

SUGGESTED READINGS

Freud, *Totem and Taboo* in *The Basic Writings of Sigmund Freud*, Random House, New York, n.d.

The Future of an Illusion, tr. by W. D. Robson-Scott, London, 1949.

Luijpen, *Phenomenology and Atheism*, Chapter Four, Section Five.

Paul Ricoeur, "The Atheism of Freudian Psychoanalysis," *Concilium*, vol. 16, 1966, pp. 59 ff.

John Bamberger, "Religion as an Illusion?," *ibid.*, pp. 73 ff.

Gregory Zilboorg, *Freud and Religion*, Westminster, 1958.

CHAPTER THREE

SOCIAL ATHEISM

For the pious believer the heavens are the theater of God's glory. But in the eyes of many atheists, God—the God of religion—is the theater of man's misery. This is particularly true of the man who is the chief topic of our considerations in this chapter, Karl Marx. His reflections upon religion find their focal point in his attention to the wretchedness to which, he holds, belief in God condemns man in his earthly life.

Like any other philosopher, Marx must be seen against the background of his time and within the context of other thinkers who influenced him. This means that a measure of attention must be paid to a few other thinkers without whom the particular form assumed by Marx's atheism cannot be properly understood. Foremost among these are Hegel and Feuerbach.

1. HISTORICAL ANTECEDENTS OF MARX'S ATHEISM

Marx was born in 1818 in Trier, Germany, from Jewish parents. His father was a lawyer who, two years before Karl's birth, became a convert to Lutheran Christianity, in order to overcome the handicap of being a Jew. Karl also was baptized when he was six years old and received religious instruction at the Gymnasium of Trier. The home atmosphere, however, remained permeated with the ideas of Voltaire and Rousseau. There is no evidence that religion ever played a positive role in his life, even before he became a professed atheist.

His mental development toward atheism began when he went to study at the University of Berlin and joined the *Doktor-Klub*, a group of Young Hegelians. As early as his doctoral dissertation, which he presented at the age of twenty-three, Marx undertook the defense of the atheism of Epicurus. But it was only after he became acquainted with the ideas of Feuerbach that Marx's atheism assumed a form of its own.

Hegelian Influences on Marx

In the *Doktor-Klub* Marx became familiar with Hegel and developed for this great thinker a respect which he never lost throughout the rest of his life. This respect, however, was not one of slavish admiration but that of a very critical mind which had recognized both the genius and some of the short-comings of Hegel. Marx took over a number of things from Hegel, while modifying most of them profoundly; for instance, Hegel's dialectics, his dynamic conception of man, and the idea of alienation. Of particular interest to us will also be the fact that Hegel demanded the individual's self-sacrifice for the sake of the universal Spirit's self-realization.

After Hegel's death in 1831, there arose two trends of Hegelian thought: the Old or Right Wing Hegelians and the Young or Left Wing Hegelians. The Old Hegelians saw the State as the infallible expression of right and morality. Unbelievable as it sounds to modern ears, they thought that man could reach authentic freedom and self-realization only by obedience to the absolute authority of the State and the legal establishment. Identifying philosophy and religion, they proceeded to support the absolute monarchy with a "religious" foundation.

The Young Hegelians of the *Doktor-Klub*, which Marx and Friedrich Engels had joined, were radically opposed to both absolute monarchy and the notion of a religious foundation for the State. They argued in favor of a "State of reason"; separation from religion—which they cordially despised—should make it possible for the State to bring about a just order of society. Soon, however, they went even further and turned against the very idea of the State, retaining only faith in humanity.

Bruno Bauer, one of the leading figures in the *Doktor-Klub*, quickly became a friend of Marx, but this friendship did not last. Bauer—a somewhat anomalous character, who had taught theology while being a professed atheist—convinced Marx that Hegel's philosophy was really atheistic. In Hegel's philosophy man and nature are absorbed by God for his own glorification; thus man and nature are rendered utterly meaningless. The Hegelian God, Bauer argued, was also the God of Christianity. For Scripture presents God as one who keeps man enslaved; man is nothing and can do nothing; God is the Alpha and Omega; he operates everything in all things. Thus man has no longer any possibility of making history; God himself is the Lord of history.

Marx was duly impressed by his friend's arguments, but less pleased by the fact that Bauer continued to cling to the idea that social reality could be transformed through "criticism," i.e., that the development and refinement of ideas would automatically transform the world. Influenced by Arnold Ruge, Marx soon turned against Bauer's actionless criticism, arguing that a philosophy which remains satisfied with sheer contemplation is an ivory tower pursuit rather than a dynamic philosophy of life.

Finally, Moses Hess also confirmed Marx in his atheism. Hess was an early defender of communism and believed that a revolution would be needed to abolish private property. But any revolution, he argued, that was carried out by believers in God was doomed to fail. In one form or another those believers would simply restore God to his throne and thus again prevent man from being himself.

Let us now see somewhat more in detail the ideas of the man who most strongly influenced Marx's atheism, Ludwig Feuerbach (1804-1872).

Feuerbach's Atheism

Feuerbach's main ideas on God and religion are contained in his THOUGHTS ABOUT DEATH AND IMMORTALITY, a work which he published anonymously at the ages of twenty-six, and his later works THE ESSENCE OF CHRISTIANITY, THE ESSENCE OF RELIGION and THE PHILOSOPHY OF THE FUTURE. Wary of Hegelian "abstractions," Feuerbach wished to think as a real living being, to "think in existence, in the world, as a part of it," and "not in a vacuum." But for Feuerbach "real being" meant "sensuous and material being, for the body in its totality is my ego, I myself."[1] This professed identification of reality with matter constitutes Feuerbach as a materialist; and as soon as all reality is identified with matter, there is of course no longer any possibility whatsoever of affirming a transcendent, supra-worldly God. Religion then becomes utterly meaningless and the affirmation of such a God can only turn man away from concern with the earth and earthly reality. As a matter of fact, Feuerbach's avowed aim was to change "the friends of God into friends of man . . . , worshippers into workers" for mankind, "Christians into whole men."[2]

For Feuerbach God and the hereafter are nothing but projections. The ideas of God and an afterlife arise in man's own mind and then certain psychological factors make man exteriorize these ideas as if they were something outside his mind in reality. Let us see how this happened according to Feuerbach.

1. *Philosophie der Zukunft,* Frommann, 1922, pp. 87, 7.
2. *Das Wesen der Religion, Sämtliche Werke,* Stuttgart, 1903 ff., vol. 8, pp. 228 f.

In his THOUGHTS ABOUT DEATH AND IMMORTALITY Feuerbach argues that man believes in immortality because he cannot bear the idea that the dead are dead. Man therefore says that they live "the life of the dead." This belief in immortality is obviously based on a "misunderstanding of human nature" and on what man wishes to be true. Yet man also shows what he really thinks about the dead. He weeps and laments while he insists that they have passed on to a better life. His very deeds show that he really knows better; otherwise why would he weep over the dead?

Belief in an afterlife is nothing but a distorted belief in an earthly life. Man generally likes his earthly life; he feels at home on the earth. That's why he is loath to recognize the reality of death and imagines that his life will be prolonged in a fancied hereafter. He changes a subjective need into an objective reality. A vague kind of belief in an afterlife antedates Christianity, but Christianity committed the crime of eliminating this vagueness and uncertainty; it promised the certainty of everlasting happiness in a better life. But in the process Christianity reduced the good life of man on earth to death. For to attain the promised better life, man must put up with the evils of his earthly life; these evils remain unchallenged, thereby diminishing or destroying the happiness of man's earthly life. Christianity is a religion of suffering.[3]

The idea of God also is a product of the imagination. God is not a subject but a predicate: dreadful, great, glorious, powerful, good, merciful. The true subject is nature, and the feelings man has about nature find expression in the predicates he ascribes to the gods. (God with a capital is nothing but the name of the species to which Zeus, Odin, Yahweh, Swantowit

---

3. *Gedanken über Tot und Unsterblichkeit, Sämtliche Werke,* vol. 1, pp. 98 f., 105 f., 116 f.

and Christ belong.) What man calls God is merely the impression nature makes on him.[4]

In THE ESSENCE OF CHRISTIANITY Feuerbach develops these ideas further. Man's own nature here is no longer merely the basis of religion but becomes its very *object.* Religion is supposed to be man's consciousness of the Infinite, but the only infinite of which man is conscious is his own infinity: man's consciousness knows no limits. Unlike the caterpillar, the consciousness of which doesn't extend beyond the kind of leaf on which it feeds, man's consciousness knows no such limitations.

Individual men recognize, of course, that they are limited, but this doesn't mean that man's essence is limited. For the only reason why the individual is conscious of his limitations lies in the fact that he has for his object the infinity of the species to which he belongs. The individual would be wrong in ascribing his own limitations to the species. He is inclined to do this, however, because in this way he need not be ashamed of his limitation; the others have it also. This is foolish, argues Feuerbach, for the limitations of any kind of being exist only in comparison with other kinds. The life of a butterfly, for example, is short only as compared to that of long-lived animals; for butterflies themselves their short life is just as long as the long life of a turtle is long for turtles. In other words, for man himself there exist no limitations; he is infinite, limitless for himself; his own being is the highest being, God.

Thus the object of religion is within man; God is man's own hidden self and religion is but the solemn unveiling of man's own hidden riches. The religious man doesn't realize at once that his first consciousness of God is consciousness of his own essence, his first consciousness of himself as man. For at first man looks at his own essence as something different than him-

4. *Ibid.*, pp. 107 f.

self; he exteriorizes it and calls it God. Only later does he discover that this God is really himself.

Historically speaking, Feuerbach says, every new, more advanced religion always rejects what its more ancient and primitive sisters adored as God. The more advanced religions disclose that the so-called superhuman contents of the older religions were after all something human, an exteriorization and personification of man's own powers. Fire was a god as long as man stood in awe of it, but no longer when man learned how to make and control it; fertility ceased to be divine when man grasped its workings.

All the attributes of God, then, are merely attributes of man's own nature, viewed as if it were a being apart from man himself. But the divine being is nothing but human nature stripped of the individual's imperfections, and then revered as if it were a distinct being. Theologians, says Feuerbach, readily concede that all attributes ascribed to God are merely attributes of man, as long as one doesn't claim that their subject is and can be only man himself. But after denying that any of those attributes fits God as their subject, they nonetheless insist on maintaining God as a subject. I am not an atheist, so those theologians say, if I reject all those attributes, but I become one if I reject their subject. But a subject without any attributes is nothing for me, it is a non-entity. If I must reject all predicates of the subject called God, then I should logically also reject the subject itself.

Some theologians, Feuerbach continues, agree that the attributes assigned to God are merely human qualities; yet they refuse to reject them. The attributes, so they argue, are meaningless with respect to God in himself but apply only to God-for-me, God-for-man. Man cannot help representing God in a human way, as similar to man, but he knows that these human qualities do not apply to God as he is in himself. This distinction between God-in-himself and God-for-me, however, says

Feuerbach, is baseless. It is absolutely impossible for me to know God-in-himself; the only concept of God I can ever have is that of God-for-me. God can only appear to man as a being resembling man because man knows nothing better than being-man.

Thus people call God wise and good because they know nothing better than being-wise and being-good; they call him love because they appreciate love. When man was still a primitive hunter, his gods dwelled in the forest, as did man himself, but when man began to live in houses, his gods also moved into temples. For warlike people God is a god of war, but for peace-loving man a god of war is a distortion of God just as war itself is a distortion of man. Briefly put, Scripture may tell us that God created man to his image and likeness, but in reality it is man who creates God to his own image and likeness. And thus as man changes, so does religion. Yesterday's religion is today's atheism, and today's atheism will be tomorrow's religion.

Another important aspect of the distinction the religious man makes between God and man is that, in order to strengthen the proclaimed lack of identity between himself and God, man must lower himself as much as possible. By projecting his own essence as an alien being called God outside himself, man strips himself of his own riches: God is all; man is nothing. In this way man is alienated from himself and no longer able to be authentically human. He makes himself an object for the projected image of himself which he calls God; he is no longer a man.[5]

We will not follow Feuerbach's further development and application of these ideas to Christianity in particular. For our purpose the preceding paragraphs sufficiently illustrate his attempts to unmask religion. Let us note, however, that Feuer-

5. *The Essence of Christianity*, pp. 12 ff.

bach's positive aim was to regain for man his authentic humanity: "I deny the fantastic projection of theology and religion," he says, "in order to affirm the real essence of man."[6] Unmasked, God reveals himself as man; unmasked, theology is anthropology. But religion doesn't wish to be unmasked; it refuses to acknowledge that its content is only human. For religion God comes first, but in reality man is first. Sooner or later people will learn to see this and then they will turn away from religion.

Christianity in particular will be rejected. For it teaches that the world has no value and is of no interest. All a Christian should think about is himself and heaven, the salvation of his soul. He is not an earthly being but "out of this world," a stranger on the earth which is the only real home man knows.[7]

If God, who according to religion holds the first place, in reality comes second because man is first, then it follows, says Feuerbach in the concluding chapter of THE ESSENCE OF CHRISTIANITY, that love for man cannot be derived from anything else: "If human nature is the highest nature to man, then practically the highest and first law must be love of man to man. *Homo homini Deus est*" (man is God for man). This love of fellowman is "the axis on which revolves the history of the world."[8] That's why worshippers must become workers for mankind, candidates for the hereafter must become students of the world, and servants of heaven free citizens of the earth.

Critical Reflections

Let us begin with some objectionable points in Feuerbach's view. It stands to reason that there is no longer any room for an authentic "affirmation" of God as soon as being-man is totally

6. *Das Wesen der Religion,* p. 14; cf. *The Essence of Christianity,* p. 27.

7. *The Essence of Christianity,* p. 66.

8. *Ibid.,* p. 271.

identified with being-in-the-world. When this identification is made—as it was by Feuerbach—there is no escape from explaining God and religion as some kind of projection. But what remains of such an explanation if God really exists? Feuerbach devotes very little attention to the question of God's existence. And what he says about it (in Chapter Twenty of THE ESSENCE OF CHRISTIANITY) merely serves to affirm his conviction that God is man's nature projected as a separate being. All this simply amounts to an *a priori* denial of God's existence.

Secondly, for Feuerbach the choice is between man and a God who prevents man from being himself, a God who alienates man from himself, a God, therefore, who appears to be in competition with man. This is not surprising, for, as we saw above, Feuerbach shows no awareness of God's transcendence, of a God who is a supraworldly reality and has given the earth to man as the domain in which he is to bring about his self-realization.

Thirdly, isn't it rather naive to identify man with God when one considers man not abstractly but as he concretely is? Is man essentially good or essentially ambivalent, capable of both good and evil? It may seem easy to get rid of God in one way or another, to make the term "God" simply stand for the God-in-man rather than a transcendent Being, but to use Nietzsche's expression, the "existence of the devil" is not thereby disproved. What we mean is this: man is both good, a lover of his fellowman, and evil, a "wolf for his fellowman" (Hobbes). If man is essentially both of these, how can one simply identify God with human nature? Feuerbach is guilty here of mystifying the reality of man.

Let us now pay attention to some of the good points in his view. We find in Feuerbach concern with the whole man. Reacting sharply to the Cartesian split, which made man a spirit attached to a body, and to the Hegelian concern with the mind or reason alone, Feuerbach emphasized—but overemphasized —that man is a bodily being living in the world. His antispiritualism is to his credit.

Feuerbach's aim to change friends of God into friends of man, worshippers into workers for mankind, Christians into whole men, may strike today's authentic Christians as strange. In their eyes authentic Christianity demands effective love of one's fellowmen as a necessary consequence of one's professed love of God; one cannot be a friend of God unless he is also a friend of man, for "faith without works" is sheer hypocrisy. Similarly, today's thoughtful Christians also equate Christian holiness with Christian wholeness: a holy man must be wholly man. But we should not forget that Feuerbach wrote at a time which was strongly influenced by neo-Platonic and Cartesian spiritualism. It was the spirit or the soul that mattered; man was essentially a spirit which somehow got entangled with a body and felt ashamed of his body.

With respect to Christianity in particular, aloofness from involvement with the world appeared to be ideal. The good Christian, according to this mentality, was the soul who fled from the world and lived a pure life unstained by contact with the world. Institutionalized Christianity remained too inactive with respect to the evil conditions resulting from the objective structures of "Christendom's" society. This statement should not be taken to mean that there were no Christian movements to combat these evil conditions. As a matter of fact, the nineteenth century saw the birth of many Christian social initiatives. We are referring only to *institutionalized* Christianity when we complain of its inertia. It is to Feuerbach's credit that he contributed to the purification of religion by emphasizing that man must be involved with his fellowmen and seriously strive to make the world a place of happiness for man.

Finally, we also agree with Feuerbach that it is impossible

for man to speak about God-in-himself; all man can do is speak about God-for-him. This is an insight that is strongly emphasized in today's existential phenomenology and widely accepted also by others. In this sense it is true that man creates God to his own image and likeness and that theology is anthropology. Man's self-understanding inevitably finds expression in his understanding of God.

To use a modern expression, in Feuerbach's time there existed a "credibility gap" with respect to the God presented by institutionalized Christianity. Religion too often served as an idiological weapon in the hands of vested interests; by stressing other-worldliness, it tended to forget man's this-worldliness. This was a point that was taken up even more strongly by the man upon whom Feuerbach had made a profound impression—Karl Marx.

2. THE ATHEISM OF KARL MARX

Marx and Feuerbach

In spite of all his admiration for Feuerbach, Marx felt compelled to criticize him for not going far enough in his analysis of religion. Feuerbach, he said, neglected the true driving force of human events, which is work and the socio-economic conditions resulting from work. While correctly conceiving religion as a projection springing from man's interiority, says Marx, Feuerbach failed to explain satisfactorily why man wishes to make such a projection. He stopped when "the chief thing still remains to be done," for man's religious self-alienation "is really only explained by the self-cleavage and self-contradictoriness" of man's earthly life.[9]

Like other materialists, says Marx, Feuerbach remained a contemplative of the world; he didn't know that man is not a

9. "Theses on Feuerbach," Marx and Engels, *Selected Works*, vol. 2, pp. 404 f. Hereafter referred to as *SW*.

detached observer but practically involved in the world; he forgot that man's essence is not an abstraction but merely "the ensemble of social relations." Thus religion is simply a "social product," a phenomenon produced by a particular form of society. The alienation of religion is caused by the general alienation of man in that form of society. Because he indulged in abstractions, Feuerbach could, on the one hand, abolish religion and, on the other, introduce a new religion, viz., man's love for his fellowmen. If he had only paid attention to the reality of life, he would have seen that it is not love but work that brings people together and gives rise to mutual bonds.[10] Real unity among men is the product of their social work, and not of the abstract universality of a specific essence. And because religion is founded on man's way of living and working together, only a critique of society can be the ultimate critique of religion.

Let us see now more in detail how Marx developed his own critique of religion. For reasons that should be obvious now, this means that we must consider also his critique of society, and this will entail a brief discussion of his entire philosophy.

Man, the Self-realizing Being

Marx's philosophy is primarily a philosophy of history, an attempt to understand "the heart of history," to determine "what makes it tick," and thus to discern the fundamental pattern underlying the course of history. Knowledge of such a pattern makes it possible to understand why past events occurred and to predict, to some extent, the future course of human history.

Before Marx, Hegel had tried to do the same. Hegel was struck by the fact that thought is both particular and universal; that is, the individual makes the judgment (e.g., "man is mor-

---

10. *Ibid.*

tal"), but he makes it as a judgment that everyone should make. Besides, no matter how many individuals make it, this judgment itself remains the same. This reflection induced Hegel to subordinate the plurality of individuals to the unity and universality of thought. Individuals were for him phases in the development of universal thought. Thus the human history of individuals and groups or nations was nothing but the history of thought on its way to full self-development. Hegel himself in this way became the privileged subject in whom history, for the first time, became conscious of itself.

Marx was profoundly impressed by the powerful unifying perspective opened up by Hegel's view and in particular by the dynamic aspect of Hegel's vision: man is not a static entity which merely repeats itself within fixed limits, but each man is a participant in a common historical process of development. To be man is to become man.

But in Marx's eyes, Hegel was too "thoughtful." For Hegel, he argued, all real, external struggles are simply changed into "pure struggles of thought," so that the "history of mankind becomes the history of the abstract spirit." That, Marx adds, is the typical attitude of an ivory tower, contemplative thinker; he makes history "stand on its head" instead of letting it walk on its feet. History doesn't walk on ideas in the head but marches on its feet, and these feet, says Marx, are the material conditions of life. In other words, to understand the course of history, we must pay attention to the development of these material conditions, and this development, Marx claims, is determined by a single factor—work. Work is the very heart of history, it makes history "tick": "The entire so-called history of the world is nothing but the begetting of man through human labor."[11]

---

11. "Private Property and Communism," *Economic and Philosophic Manuscripts of 1844*, Moscow, n.d., pp. 113 f. Hereafter referred to as *MS*.

Man humanizes himself by working and he works when he makes nature the object of his activity. At first he merely used the forces of his body to work, but gradually he looked for extensions of himself by picking up stones for grinding and crushing and sharp bones for piercing things. Thus he learned to use and fabricate, first, tools and then increasingly more sophisticated instruments. History can be divided into periods according to the development of man's toolmaking ability. The better his tools, the more progress there is in man's self-realization.

Moreover, work is not only man's way of becoming more authentically man, but also conditions his co-existence with his fellowmen. To reach a level of authentic human existence, people must work together and for one another. For then they can have a division of labor and force nature to yield a greater surplus, so that the world will be more available to man and allow him to realize his potential. Thus work not merely makes man a man but also a fellowman, a member of human society. This fellowship ties the individual to all of his fellowmen through the unifying bond of work and the means of work: every new generation begins with the productive forces of the preceding generation and develops them further. When it passes away, it hands over its productive forces to the next generation. The whole of history, then, owes its coherence to work; it becomes progressively more a history of human co-existence as the means of production reach greater development.[12]

Work is for Marx the central reference point of his philosophy, for everything else is seen in the light of work and the resultant development of the means of production. A certain economic structure arises from this development, and this eco-

12. "Letter to Annenkov," *SW*, vol. 2, p. 442.

nomic infrastructure determines everything else, viz., the social, political and legal order, as well as man's "forms of consciousness," i.e., the way he thinks about himself, family, religion, art, science, philosophy, etc.[13] Let us investigate this point somewhat more in detail.

Isolated farming families produced virtually everything for themselves; they grew their own food on their own land, spun their own wool, made their own clothes, etc. Owner, worker and consumer were identical. Such a self-sufficient family met other people as equally self-sufficient families. But when specialization began through a division of labor, a few people did all the weaving, others all the tailoring, woodworking, etc. While each one still owned the tools of his trade, people worked for one another and they began to meet as customers and suppliers of home-made goods. With the introduction of textile-mills and other forms of large-scale industry, this situation changed again. Someone owned the mill but he himself did not operate the machinery; and those who worked for him did not own the mill. This development of the means of production thus gave rise to new categories of people: non-working owners and non-owning workers. The economic situation is, of course, much more complex than this simple example suggests, yet it can serve to illustrate Marx's claim that the development of the means of production determines the relations man has with his fellowmen.

The economic infrastructure rather than any kind of "political or religious nonsense," says Marx, determines the social bonds among men. As the means of production develop, they acquire a character that is no longer in harmony with the prevailing system of ownership. A box of tools, for example, can be

13. "Preface to the Critique of Political Economy," *SW*, vol. 1, p. 362 f.

a worker's private property, but a factory is by its very nature a social means of production: it is operated by many and produces for many; hence it should not be privately owned. But if this happens anyhow, conflicts arise between owner and worker. This conflict is fought on every level—legal, political, religious, aesthetic and philosophical—but these levels merely represent the superstructure built on the economic infrastructure. The economic situation is reflected as in a mirror on these levels.

For instance, the legal order regulates the production, distribution and exchange of goods, but all this order really does is raise the position of those who are economically strong to the rank of law. It makes their will an obligation for all. And the political order merely adds the power of the State to reinforce the position of those who rule.

Philosophy and religion also are economically determined. For the group which "is the ruling material force of society is at the same time its ruling intellectual force."[14] The thinkers of this group simply give expression to the situation resulting from the prevailing socio-economic conditions which favor them. Morality, religion and philosophy do not lead an autonomous life but are merely mirror images reflecting the development of the means of production. Man's consciousness, that is, his way of thinking about himself, society, etc., is determined by being, i.e., the material conditions of existence.

Man's Self-alienation in a Capitalistic Society

Examining the society of his time in the light of his fundamental principles, Marx came to the conclusion that in every realm of life the capitalistic structure of society makes it impossible for man to realize himself authentically. He can only

14. Marx and Engels, *The German Ideology*, International Publishers, New York, 1947, p. 39.

lead an estranged or alienated existence is such a society. Let us see what Marx means by self-estrangement.

Marx borrowed this term from Hegel but modified it to fit his own materialistic perspective. For Hegel also man's essence is work but, says Marx, the only work Hegel knows is abstract mental work; hence for Hegel man's self-expression lies on the spiritual level. At first, however, man fails to recognize himself in his self-expressions; they appear alien to him, "other than himself," estranged from him. To overcome his self-alienation, man must return to himself on a higher level of thought.

Marx modified this Hegelian idea of alienation by transferring it to the level of man's dynamic being in the world. Man's self-expression thus lies in his being at work in the world. There he is estranged from his self-expression, not because his mind fails to recognize itself its products, but because he is in a material way prevented from being himself in his work and deprived from the product of his activity: the capitalistic order of society forces him to sell himself for wages and takes the product of his work, which is his self-expression, away from him. The only way this self-estrangement can be overcome, says Marx, is by the abolition of capitalistic society, for then work can be humanized and the product of man's work can be restored to him. Because man is self-estranged in the economic infrastructure which determines everything else, he is also self-estranged in all other dimensions of life.

The meaning of the terms "self-alienation" and "self-estrangement" can be clarified by means of the contemporary ideas of authenticity and inauthenticity. Man and things human are authentic when they are what they ought to be; they are inauthentic when they are not what they ought to be. Speech, for example, is authentic when it is an expression of what I personally see and experience, but inauthentic when it is meaningless chatter, a mere repetition of what "everyone" says (Heidegger). A meeting with a fellowman is an authentic encounter when we meet as true persons, but inauthentic when we see each other merely as means to obtain something. Man, then, is self-estranged if he does not live up to what he "has to be," when he realizes himself in a way that goes counter to the integral fundamental orientation of his being-man. Let us see now why, according to Marx, capitalism estranges man economically and, in consequence of this, on all levels of life.

Capitalism essentially is a system in which private individuals own and control for their own profit social means of production, that is, means of production which are operated by many and produce for the consumption of many. The reason why the private owner can make a profit is that the workers' activity increases the value of the raw materials, but the owner pays the workers less than the value they add by their work. In other words, profit simply is unpaid labor.

Abstracting from the *actual* misery caused by this exploitation of the worker, let us consider the *essential* evil of the system. For Marx man is essentially a worker, a being who humanizes himself by his work and for whom work is *the way* of being a man. But by being forced to work for a wage, man has to sell himself as a worker, he makes his life activity a "mere means of existence." Thus, by reducing his very life to nothing but a means to live, he becomes self-estranged. That's why under a capitalistic regime the worker doesn't feel "at home" in his work and shuns it "like the plague" whenever possible. He feels dehumanized by his work. His self-estrangement as a worker clearly manifests itself in the fact that his capitalistic owner takes away the product of his work.[15]

This economic self-alienation of man determines also his co-existence with his fellowmen on the social, juridical and political levels; he is unable to co-exist authentically with his fellow-

15. "Estranged Labor" *MS*, pp. 69 f.

men and is estranged from them. The worker can see the owner only as one who robs him of his existence as a human being, and vice versa. "Having" replaces "being" in a capitalistic society. The worker is looked upon as a mere means to having more money, more profit. His personal value as a human being is negated; he is reduced to a mere thing, a factor in a productive process. In the same perverted way the thing called "money" becomes endowed with all the respect that ought to be given to a person. And I am regarded as "somebody" not for what I am but for what I have. Thus capitalism turns everything into its contrary; it alienates everything from what it really is.[16]

Moreover, in a capitalistic society the people are divided into classes, groups conscious of the fact that their economic conditions put them in opposition to other groups. The capitalistic system not only estranges the workers from the capitalistic owners, but also pits capitalist against capitalist in their struggle for more profit. In addition, it causes the workers in their wretchedness to compete among themselves for sheer survival and allows them merely the negative solidarity of common suffering through common self-estrangement.[17] Even family life is self-estranged. Bourgeois families marry on the basis of dowry and inheritance, so as to increase their capital. And in the marriage of proletarians the woman is forced to sell herself as a worker for sheer survival; besides, she is looked upon as the producer of new workers, particularly in the form of cheap child labor. Thus family life is estranged by the capitalistic system.[18]

This same system ratifies the privileges of the bourgeois and their oppression of the poor by society's legal order. Its so-

16. "The Meaning of Human Requirements," *MS*, pp. 115 ff.; "The Power of Money in Bourgeois Society," *MS*, pp. 137 ff.

17. "Wage Labor and Capital," *SW*, vol. 1, pp. 102 ff.

18. Marx and Engels, *Manifesto of the Communist Party*, Moscow, n.d., pp. 53, 82 f.

called "sacred rights" of personal freedom and private property are nothing but a mystification of the capitalist's will to preserve his ill-gotten goods for himself alone. Authentic freedom is beyond the reach of the workers, whose freedom is curtailed in the name of "public safety"; and "sacred private property" is meaningless to the nine-tenth of the population who have nothing. The objective course of history demands that social means of production be socially owned; in a capitalistic society they are privately owned and protected as such by law; therefore, the legal order is estranged, out of harmony with the reality of life.[19]

Similarly, the political order defended by Hegel is estranged. Authentic freedom is supposed to be reached by submission to the authority of the State, which externally unifies the people. But, argues Marx, real unity must come from within, from the people themselves; it cannot be externally imposed. Moreover, the State's claim to express the people's unity and defend their common interest is a lie. For in a capitalistic society the people are divided into warring classes, and as long as this is the case, no amount of specious theorizing can really establish unity. Siding with the privileged class against the workers, the State utters lofty phrases of being "of the whole people" and "for the whole people" but all this simply serves to camouflage the fact that the power of the State means "the power of capital over labor," brute force "organized for social enslavement." The worker, then, has no country, no fatherland to which he owes any allegiance. Any call to serve the country is merely a call to lay down his life for the defense of the oppressors' privileges. When privileged classes are removed through the abolition of capitalism, there will no longer be any need for a State to camouflage the fact that the people as a whole are divided and estranged from one another.[20]

19. *Ibid.*, pp. 79 ff.

20. "The Civil War in France," *SW*, vol. 1, p. 517; *Manifesto*, p. 84.

Philosophy also is estranged in a capitalistic society. Every philosopher tries to discover unity in the plurality of the world and express this unity in well-ordered and harmoniously connected ideas. But the real world of capitalistic society in which the philosopher lives is an alienated world of disorder, division and antagonisms, a world without order and harmony. However, the mentality of such a society doesn't permit the philosopher to express that world as it really is; that's why he turns away from it and takes refuge in the realm of abstraction. And there he then spins beautiful metaphysical fancies, instead of enlightening us about man and his real world. Such an alienated philosopher is like a man who thinks that he can save people from drowning by knocking the idea of gravity out of their head. To be authentic, philosophy should pay attention to what people really *are* and not to what they think or intend. And what people really are is determined by their socio-economic situation.[21]

Religion also is a manifestation of man's fundamental socio-economic alienation. But before discussing Marx's position with respect to religion, let us first see how he envisions man's liberation from his estrangements in the society that will arise after the destruction of capitalism.

The Coming of the Authentic Man: Communist Society

Marx did not limit himself to a critique of capitalistic society. He thought that he had discovered what makes history "tick," the fundamental laws governing the course of history with an ironclad necessity. Knowledge of these laws made it possible

21. Marx and Engels, *The Holy Family*, Moscow, 1956, pp. 15, 111; *The German Ideology*, p. 2.

for him to predict in broad lines the course of future events. He very definitely did not wish to play the prophet announcing the unknown future, nor the idealist who tries to adjust reality to his ideals. In his own eyes, he was merely a privileged witness, who happened to stand at the right place when enough of the pieces of history fell into place to see the outline of the whole picture. This outline is, according to Marx, that the authentic man will emerge from all his alienations through the victory of the proletarians over capitalistic society. Man will then be integrally human, that is wholly social.[22]

Capitalism will drive itself economically to its own dissolution, says Marx, by virtue of the "natural laws of capitalistic production." These laws are the following:

1. The surplus value of labor tends to fall in the capitalistic system. The surplus value is the difference between labor cost and the value which labor adds to the product; it is the profit margin, which arises from underpaid labor. This surplus value must necessarily decrease because the capital which must be invested for maintenance, improvement and expansion continues to increase. Thus the profit margin goes down. Intense competition forces all capitalists to ever increasing investments, so that all make less and less profit. The point where the profit margin is reduced to zero inevitably must be reached.[23]

2. Capitalism tends to concentrate on large-scale production, thereby eliminating small productive units. In addition, it tends to centralize capital into the hands of ever fewer individuals; the smaller capitalists are expropriated by the larger ones. Thus the number of capitalists tends to diminish and that of proletarians keeps growing.[24]

---

22. "Private Property and Communism," *MS*, p. 103.
23. *Capital*, Moscow, 1961 f., vol. 3, pp. 208 f.
24. *Capital*, vol. 1, pp. 762 f.

3. Motivated by profit alone, capitalism tends to overproduce. This leads to commercial crises which return periodically in ever more threatening forms. The capitalistic attempts to solve this problem merely aggravate it. They search for new markets and more thoroughly exploit the existing ones, but this merely draws more people into the destructive cycle of crises.[25]

4. As capital expands, pauperization increases. For greater mechanization and simplification of labor means that more workers will compete for fewer jobs at lower wages.[26]

The end result will be that a handful of exceedingly wealthy capitalists will own all the means of production, while the immense majority of men will be reduced to the condition of starving proletarians who "have nothing to lose but their chains." Society will then resemble a giant inverted pyramid, a structure that must inevitably collapse under its own weight. Dispossessed of everything, the proletarians have no private interest whatsoever: no property, no home, no family, no country, in any meaningful sense of these terms. As such, they are ripe for a world-wide authentically human society based on common interest alone.

And they alone will bring about this new society by a violent revolution; an authentically human existence "can be attained only by the forcible overthrow of all existing social conditions." For capitalists are motivated by profit alone; hence any attempts at reconciliation would merely be an effort to make it appear that things are changing while in reality everything remains more or less the same. The proletarians would simply be cheated out of their rights.[27]

To be successful in their revolution, the workers must first

25. *Manifesto*, p. 59.

26. "Wage Labor and Capital," *SW*, vol. 1, pp. 104 f.

27. *Manifesto*, p. 114.

constitute themselves as a class, conscious of its position *vis-à-vis* the bourgeois. It is here that the Communist Party can lead all other workers. Having no private interest to defend, the Party always and everywhere represents all workers; besides, it has over all others the advantage of clearly understanding the course of history.[28] The new society founded by the proletarians, however, will be for the benefit of all people and not merely for the workers alone. And once the new society is firmly established, each man will be able to lead an authentically human life, for there will be no alienations.

Economic estrangement, as we saw, is the foundation from which all of man's alienations arise; hence the elimination of the capitalistic economic structure is the fundamental law of Marx's coming society. All social means of production will be owned by society, so that no one will have to work as a wage slave for the private interest of others. In a bourgeois social order individual and society are seen as opposites; because private property dominates everything, *my* interest conflicts with the common interest. But when I no longer have any private interest, only the common interest continues to exist, so that "the individual is the social being." This identification of individual and society also means that the worker no longer has to sell his power to work; he now works for himself, but as a social being. He doesn't receive any wages in the old sense, but contributes to society "according to his ability" and receives from it "according to his needs."[29]

Hegel liked the universal and spoke of the human species, but he stayed in the realm of abstraction. In reality, says Marx, the species is society, man's total bond with his fellowmen.

---

28. *Ibid.*, p. 73.

29. "Private Property and Communism," *MS*, p. 105; "Critique of the Gotha Programme," *SW*, vol. 2, p. 24.

Consciousness of this total bond means that the individual no longer sees himself in opposition to the totality, the species. Individual life and the life of the species are not different but only distinct modalities of the same life. When man is authentically conscious of himself as the social being he is, the individual is nothing but a sample of the species.[30]

Having become totally social, man, says Marx, will no longer seek self-realization in "having" but in "being," in being a whole man together with and for his fellowmen. And when this universal brotherhood has been achieved, all class-consciousness will disappear, including that of the proletarian class. All that will remain is a general "association" of men in which "the free development of each is the condition for the free development of all." In the new classless society there will, of course, continue to be different functions, but they will be regulated by the community and not by an impersonal system of property relations. And since individual and society have become one, each man can freely pursue whatever sphere of activity he prefers. Having become wholly social, I will not abuse this freedom to the detriment of others.[31]

There will still be laws in the new society, but they will no longer alienate man because there will no longer be a ruling class which can present "its interest as the common interest of all." Laws will be in harmony with what man really is. Moreover, the people will not see the law as an externally imposed restraint but as the consciously formulated and freely accepted expression of social man's understanding of reality; people themselves will regulate their relationship with nature and with one another.[32] The State—which is *per se* an instrument of oppression and an alienation—will continue to exist only during the initial period of transition from the capitalistic society in

---

30. "Private Property and Communism," *MS*, pp. 104 f.
31. *Ibid.*, p. 104.
32. *The German Ideology*, p. 41; *Capital*, vol. 3, p. 800.

the form of the dictatorship of the proletariat. But once the new society is solidly established, the State will wither away, to be replaced by an organ that is "completely subordinate" to the people.[33]

In the new society thinking will continue to be a mirror reflex of socio-economic conditions. But these conditions will then be what they ought to be; hence philosophy and other forms of thought will no longer be estranged but the authentic expression of what nature and man are. Religion also will vanish because it is nothing but an expression of man's fundamental economic alienation in the old forms of society.

Let us see now more in detail Marx's position with respect to God and religion.

Marx and God

Throughout his massive works Marx pays very little attention to a serious consideration of the question whether God exists or not. He devotes a few short paragraphs to the classical proofs for God's existence in the notes attached to his doctoral dissertation. After calling them "empty tautologies," he rejects in his own way the so-called ontological proof. This proof argues as follows. God is that than which nothing can be greater. Now, the concept of that than which nothing can be greater necessarily implies existence, for otherwise something greater could be conceived—namely, everything you have included in your concept plus existence. Therefore, God exists of necessity. Marx rejects this argument as fallacious.[34]

In his ECONOMIC AND PHILOSOPHICAL MANUSCRIPTS OF 1844 Marx devotes a few lines to the idea of a Creator God. He begins by pointing out that "the creation of the earth has received a mighty blow from geogeny," that is, the sciences which study

33. "Critique of the Gotha Programme," SW, vol. 2, pp. 34 ff.

34. "Notes to the Doctoral Dissertation," *Writings of the Young Marx on Philosophy and Society*, Doubleday, 1967, pp. 65 f.

the formation of the earth, and that spontaneous generation is "the only practical refutation of the theory of creation." He then argues that the entire question of creation is meaningless. One who asks about creation, so his argument runs, must begin by supposing a situation in which nature and man do not yet exist. But this very supposition removes the questioner from the scene, and together with him the question also vanishes. By removing everything, you leave nothing; hence your question is nothing but a meaningless abstraction; it cannot be raised seriously.[35]

That's all the attention Marx pays to the question of God's existence. Leaving a discussion of the value which his meagre remarks may have for later, let us see if his followers have done any better in this matter.

Friedrich Engels, Marx's close friend and collaborator, adds very little to what Marx had said. Purposivity or finality in nature, he holds, should be explained as a physical or chemical process, for otherwise one would have to admit a "purposive Creator, God." Likewise, matter must always have been in motion, for otherwise there is no escape from admitting that motion started through an "impulse from outside," it could not be explained without God. In other words, Engels starts from the *a priori* premise that God must not be accepted.[36]

If we look at Lenin's work on religion, we find the same phenomenon. God is simply the product of man's fears, and even the most refined defense of God's existence is nothing but an attempt to justify the bourgeois' oppression of the workers.[37]

Michel Verret, a contemporary French Marxist, rejects a Creator God because God is supposed to be a pure spirit and there-

35. "Private Property and Communism," *MS*, pp. 112 f.
36. Engels, *Anti-Dühring*, 2nd ed., Moscow, 1959, pp. 86, 102.
37. Lenin, *Ueber die Religion*, Berlin, 1960, pp. 23 f., 50.

fore doesn't have any hands to make things; and if he is assumed to make things without using hands, he is nothing but a magician.[38] That's all there is among orthodox Marxists as a positive justification of their atheism.

In all justice we must add that today there are also Marxists who refuse to follow the classical Party line and show a positive appreciation of religion. For instance, Roger Garaudy holds that Marxism must enrich itself with what is best in the Christian heritage and rejects God as an alienation only because he prevents man from being himself by subjecting him to externally imposed eternal moral laws.[39] This is a very interesting development, but this issue will be discussed in connection with Nietzsche.

Let us see now why, according to Marx, so many people continue to believe in a God whose existence has been disposed of by science. As we mentioned already, Marx agrees with Feuerbach that the idea of God is nothing but a projection. Unlike Feuerbach, however, Marx explains why man makes this projection. Religion is a phenomenon belonging to a particular form of society, viz., a society in which man is prevented from being himself on earth. Religion and its God are "social products" of a society in which man is alienated from himself.

Religion as Self-alienation

Even in his earliest scholarly work, his doctoral dissertation, Marx resolutely rejects God. In the notes attached to his thesis he speaks about Prometheus, the mythical hero who stole the fire from the gods and gave it to man. Being in possession of fire, man was able to help himself by transforming things; he

38. Verret, *Les Marxistes et la religion*, Paris (1961), p. 41.

39. *The Christian Marxist Dialogue*, ed. by Paul Oestreicher, Macmillan, 1969, p. 144.

no longer needed to depend on the benevolence of the gods. Infuriated by this threat of human autonomy, Zeus issued an ultimatum: either return the fire to the gods or be forever chained to a rock and tortured by a vulture devouring your liver. Siding with Prometheus, Marx wrote: "I hate all gods," and he agreed with the hero's proud reply: "'I can assure you that I'll never exchange my miserable lot for slavery. I prefer to remain chained to this rock rather than become a vile slave of Zeus.' Prometheus ranks first among the saints and martyrs in the calendar of philosophy."[40]

The dilemma, then, is clear according to Marx: we must choose between man as a free self-realizing being and a God who wishes to keep man in the bondage of slavery. God prevents man from being himself; therefore, religion is inhuman, an inauthentic way of being-man, for it raises "an alien being above nature and above man." And because God estranges man from himself, doesn't allow him to be a "whole man," it is not enough to be merely an atheist, but one must become a militant anti-theist: "The criticism of religion ends with the doctrine that man is the highest being for man, hence with the categorical imperative to overthrow all conditions in which man is a degraded, enslaved, neglected, contemptible being."[41]

The critique of religion, however, according to Marx's fundamental principles, is a critique of "the valley of tears" which society is. Man as he really is exists only in the world and it is there that he must realize himself. But the divisions existing in society make it impossible for him to humanize himself. That's why man invents religion as an answer to his socio-economic distress: Religion is man's self-realization in his imagination,

40. MEGA ed. of works by Marx and Engels, vol. 1, part 1, Berlin, 1927, p. 10.

41. "Private Property and Communism," *MS*, p. 114; "Toward the Critique of Hegel's Philosophy of Law," *Writings of the Young Marx*, pp. 257 f.

because man's being has no authentic reality on earth. He fancies that he will be happy hereafter because he cannot be happy here. The reason why he is unhappy here lies in man's fundamental alienation on the economic level. Society, as we saw, is governed by private interests in which "having" replaces "being" and the have-nots must sell themselves just to stay alive. Religion is but an echo of this economic slavery.[42]

Like a drug-addict, unhappy man seeks consolation for his wretchedness in a dream-land: "Religion is the opium of the people." Opiates don't really remove the addict's misery but merely make him temporarily forget his woes. In a similar way religion consoles man over his wretchedness. It doesn't really remove man's unhappiness but makes him temporarily forget about it. But just as the addict must stop using drugs if he is ever to overcome his real misery, so also "the abolition of religion as people's illusory happiness is the demand for their real happiness."[43]

Religion, then, is not a harmless drug but positively dangerous. It reduces its victims to inertia, so that they don't take any steps to put an end to their real misery. Man's authentic selfhood as a human being can only be attained on the basis of an "annihilated and superseded religion." He must give up his "opium," put his shoulder to the plow and start working for the abolition of his misery by the overthrow of the material conditions from which his unhappiness arises. The sacred figure of God in his heaven is but an unholy figure of man's self-alienation though his socio-economic estrangement. It is this estrangement that is the "condition which needs illusions." To get rid of "theological inhumanity," to make authentic "human beings" of religious people, we must start the task of "abolishing the inhumanity of today's praxis of life." Man has no other god than himself.[44]

---

42. "Toward the Critique" etc., *op. cit.*, pp. 250 f.

43. *Ibid.*

44. *The Holy Family*, pp. 125, 148.

Aside from paralyzing man's efforts to get rid of oppression by lulling him into a drugged sleep, religion is also a powerful instrument of oppression in the hands of the ruling class. This applies in particular to Christianity. "The social principles of Christianity," says Marx, "upheld slavery in Antiquity, glorified serfdom in the Middle Ages and, if necessary, know how to approve the oppression of the proletariat, albeit with a sorrowful face." It gladly hands the oppressed peasant a "mortgage on heaven" to guarantee the bourgeois exploiter's mortgage on the peasant's earthly possessions. It teaches oppressed people to be resigned to "God's will," to wait patiently for their heavenly reward, and it promises them that their evils will be avenged—after they are dead. But Christianity merely admonishes the evildoers to practice charity and to return to the poor, out of the goodness of their hearts, part of what they have stolen from them. It does nothing to put an end to the nefarious oppression which the privileged few have made into laws ruling society.[45]

Thus Christianity abandons the dispossessed to the merciless pity of their oppressors; the leaders of the Churches, the " 'holy ones' show their Christianity by the humility with which they bear the overwork, the privation and the hunger of others."[46] Christianity makes God's will guarantee the social order, but in reality this order is nothing but the product of man's own work. Man, not God, makes society what it is.

Here, again, the official or orthodox followers of Marx add little to his considerations. For Lenin the powerlessness of the exploited produces faith in God and the hereafter just as in-

45. MEGA ed., vol. 1, part 6, p. 271; "The Class Struggle in France," SW, vol. 1, p. 18; *The Holy Family*, p. 249.

46. *Capital*, vol. 1, p. 265 note.

evitably as the impotence of the primitive hunter makes him believe in gods, spirits and miracles. All religion is nothing but an organ of bourgeois reaction; it comforts the oppressed with the hope of an eternal reward in order to keep him quiet. At the same time, it offers admission tickets to heaven at a reduced rate to the oppressors: they are allowed to go on oppressing the poor as long as they are charitable. What an opium![47]

For Michel Verret God is the celestial policeman who safeguards the established order; in other words, he is the servant of the establishment, the ruling class; he is a conservative, a reactionary. But his all-seeing eye watches the oppressed; he will punish all crimes against the established order. Thus the poor must continue to suffer. They are told to be resigned and hope for their heavenly fatherland; they must fight against their own needs and desires for a more decent life, for "blessed are the poor."[48]

Let us add again that some non-orthodox Marxist show more openness to the positive value of religion and the contributions it can make to man's humanity.[49]

In summary, God's existence has been disposed of by the progress of science. Belief in God alienates man from himself and his fellowmen. This alienation is merely a reflex of man's fundamental economic alienation through the private ownership of the social means of production. Man will overcome all his alienations, including religion, when he positively overcomes his economic estrangement. Religion acts as an opiate in those who believe in God because it causes them to seek happiness in a dream-land. It is also an instrument of oppression at the service of the ruling class, which preaches that the existing

47. *Ueber die Religion*, pp. 6-24.

48. *Les Marxistes et la religion*, pp. 15 f.

49. Cf. the Marxist contributions to the *Christian Marxist Dialogue*.

social order is willed by God. But man himself is the author of the social order; that's why he must change it to conform to what it ought to be.

3. CRITICAL CONSIDERATIONS

Marx, as we saw, was an atheist even before he developed his own philosophy, but he incorporated his atheism into it and it is as an integral aspect of his philosophy that his atheism ought to be considered. For this reason it will be necessary to present here not only an evaluation of his atheism but also a critical consideration of his entire philosophy. First, however, we must answer an objection that could easily be raised against a seemingly glaring omission.

No reference was made, so the objection goes, to other passages of Marx which contradict much of what we have said above. Now, a thinker who often contradicts himself is unimportant; he doesn't know what he is talking about. Such a man may be a powerful rabble-rouser but he doesn't deserve serious attention as a philosopher.

This objection is not without merit although we cannot accept its conclusion. Today no one pays attention to Adolf Hitler as a thinker; his importance was wholly based on his command of power. But many thinkers, even in the free West, continue to study Marx's philosophy by their own free choice. This fact shows that there must be something of value in his thought. Some, like Merleau-Ponty, do not hesitate to call him a classical philosopher.

A classical philosopher is a thinker who was first to see something of lasting importance and thus enabled others to see the same. But no one literally takes over what the classical philosopher first saw because he expressed his discovery in an exaggrated way. Taken literally in its original expression, a classical philosophy may be as valueless as a cancelled five-cent stamp. But in its core, in what it saw, this same philosophy is so valuable that no serious thinker can disregard it.

For example, no one will hold with Plato that the soul once lived in a world of universal ideas, that this world is the only really real world, that for some obscure reason the soul was banished from that world and incarcerated in a body, where it is now trying to remember its world of ideas. But the original vision underlying Plato's words is the spiritual aspect of man, and this is something which no serious thinker can disregard with impunity. Similarly, the materialistic view that man is nothing but matter, nothing but a thing disregards the fact that man is a subject, one who gives meaning to himself and to things. Yet, whoever neglects the original vision underlying materialism—the idea that man is whatever he is on the basis of matter—presents a distorted picture of man.

In a similar way Marx may be viewed as a classical philosopher; he cannot be disregarded with impunity, yet he should not be followed literally. The reason why should become evident in the following pages. Let us now first present a few general reflections on his philosophy and then a special consideration of his atheism and his critique of religion.

General Remarks About Marx's Philosophy

The nineteenth century witnessed many efforts to get rid of Cartesian dualism, the split between mind or soul and body and between subject and world. Marx was one of those who took part in the battle against this split and deserves credit for pointing out that ideas do not arise in a vacuum but are born in a historical situation. He goes too far, however, when he claims that not ideas ("the head") but the material conditions ("the feet") determine the course of history. Both together determine history, for the material conditions are not what they are for me independently of the ideas in my head. The meaning of those conditions for me depends on the project of self-realization in my head. By disregarding this interdependence in his theory, Marx fell into the trap of Cartesianism which he had wanted to avoid.

Secondly, Marx rightly emphasized that man is a dynamic being who must realize himself in the world through his activity. But he exaggerated the importance of work—in the sense of productive labor—when he made man nothing but a worker. Work, for Marx, was not a means of living, not *a* way of life, but *the* way. We should grant him that work is not a *mere* means of living and that it is *a* way of life. It is a way of life, just as eating, playing and loving are ways of life. And because it is a way of life, it must be performed under conditions worthy of man. At the same time, work remains also a means of living, for the other ways of life can be pursued only if through work man makes these other ways of life possible for himself.

Marx is right again when he emphasizes the social aspect of work, that by working with and for others people can reach an authentic level of humanity. Man indeed is essentially a social being. But Marx absolutizes this truth again when he makes co-existence *as workers* something which will guarantee authentic humanity. The possibility of hatred and indifference is not eliminated by the fact that I know that my work will benefit the others.

It must also be granted that the idea of work as a central reference point throws a surprising light on the course of history and led Marx to the discovery of "necessary" lines of development in history and society. But living in an era in which "necessity" was still equated with the determinism of physical science, Marx interpreted his discovery in the deterministic sense. This led him to the unjustifiable claim that the authentic man would of necessity come about by the socialization of the means of production.

With respect to the superstructure built on the economic foundation, Marx was right in emphasizing the enormous power of socio-economic "structures" over our thinking. But it was only by disregarding the presence of the subject with his ideas, aims and intentions in these structures that Marx could claim that the infrastructure exercises a deterministic influence on the superstructures. That's why for him the social, legal and political order are nothing but mirror images of the economic situation and why man's way of thinking about himself and the world is simply a reflex of this situation. Scientism—which was perhaps unavoidable in his time—made him pattern his theory on the model of physical science and disregard the presence of man as a giver of meaning in the infrastructure.

In spite of all these shortcomings, it remains true that Marx made a fundamental discovery, viz., the material substratum of existence plays an important role in all of life's dimensions. Man is whatever he only on the basis of matter. He can come to an authentically human existence only by really humanizing the world; his self-development is contingent on his development of the earth.

Marx's analysis of the capitalistic society of his time strikes us as, in the main, correct, but here, too, he disregards the power of the subject to change the economic project. Owners can temper their attitude of "greed" with concern for the workers as fellowmen and introduce structures to safeguard the human dignity of all. In other words, they need not of necessity look upon workers as nothing but thinglike forces of production; they need not of necessity be nothing but seekers of profit, no matter what the cost to others. Marx rightly criticized the society of his time for not being concerned with the worker's self-realization as a human being, but wrongly claimed that, as long as private ownership prevails, workers are of necessity reduced to things.

Marx also deserves credit for his refusal to let the evil conditions be remedied by the practice of individual charity. Giving alms is no substitute for society's failure to do justice to all people as human beings. Such a failure means that authentic love of fellowmen doesn't find the social expression it ought to have. The structures of society must be such that authentic self-realization is *really* open to all.

With respect to the new society to be established by the proletarians, Marx fails to offer convincing arguments why only a violent revolution can succeed in bringing about the desired changes. As a matter of fact, most of the steps he proposed for the period of transition between capitalism and the new society have actually been introduced in the advanced nations of the West without any violent revolution. Yet we must credit Marx with clearly seeing that authentic humanity demanded profound changes. Our present awareness of man's social dimension owes much to Marx.

An entirely different matter, however, is whether the transfer of the social means of production from private hands to ownership by society can make man transcend his alienation and become authentically human. "Society owns the factories" is a hollow phrase, for society cannot *really* act as owner. Real ownership means the ability to exercise effective control, and this control society would have to exercise through individuals acting on its behalf. But what is there to guarantee that these individuals will keep their hands unstained by private interests? Absolute guarantees cannot be given where people rather than things are concerned. Yet Marx tries to convince us that the structure of the new society will be such a guarantee.

Marx rightly objected to the Hegelian idea that authentic freedom consists in submitting to the dictates of the State's absolute power and that, by doing this, the individual would attain full self-realization. But he demands that everyone submit to the absolute dictates of his theory about the new society because its premises are supposedly guaranteed by scientific reason. Besides, Marx's idea of the new social man reduces the individual to a mere sample copy of the species and denies him any unique and unreplaceable value of his own. Can I be authentically myself if I am nothing but a sample of a common essence?

There are many other points that can be raised, but these few remarks may suffice in the present context. Let us now consider more extensively Marx's standpoint with respect to God and religion.

Marx and the Existence of God

Marx, we saw, rejects the so-called ontological argument for God, and he is right. But, following Thomas Aquinas, the immense majority of Christian philosophers has always done the same. The argument, most of them hold, is a logical fallacy. The only valid conclusion it allows is that *if* God exists, he exists of necessity. But as it stands, the argument jumps from the logical order to the ontological order, from ideas to reality.

Secondly, Marx's argument against a Creator God begins by assuming that one must choose between either creation or the findings of the earth sciences, that creation and scientific theory are competing explanations of the same phenomenon, and that God hides somewhere in a dark corner unexplored as yet by science. But philosophy and positive science are not mutually exclusive, competing theories, but move on different levels. Nothing any cosmological science will ever discover about the physical formation of the earth or the universe contributes anything to the philosophical problem of the world's creation. Reversely, as we saw in Chapter One, God is a useless hypothesis in any attempt to answer physical questions about the universe.

Let us keep in mind, however, that the critical examination of what physical science can and cannot do had not yet been performed in Marx's time. His argument may have seemed to carry some weight in an era dominated by the imperialism of physical science.

Marx also gratuitously assumes that creation answers a non-existent question because it inquires, so he says, into the origin of the universe at a time when the universe and the questioner did not yet exist. He takes for granted that once something is "there," its existence raises no philosophical problems. This is a sophomoric assumption. It is precisely the fact that there really exist beings which do not have within themselves a sufficient reason for their actual existence that gives rise to the idea of creation.

The question, then, about creation is not a pseudo-question raised by a questioner before he exists but is raised by the questioner precisely insofar as he finds himself and the universe existing; it is not a question for a non-existent subject but for an existent subject. The only point where Marx is right here is that all questions—and all affirmations—always refer to the subject who questions or affirms. In the language of existential phenomenology, "is" always refers to the subject who affirms, being is being-for-man.

Marx's glib disposal of the question of God's existence shows that the matter was already decided for him *a priori.* Let us add that his atheism did not flow from his philosophy of history and society. He had already opted for atheism before he developed his philosophy. But later he incorporated his view of religion as an alienation into his theory, making it a mirror image of man's fundamental economic estrangement.

God and Man's Self-realization

Man can only be man if he rejects any kind of God above him. He can realize himself as an authentic human being only if he is his own God. It is this conviction rather than any dissatisfaction with the metaphysical proofs for God's existence that underlies Marx's atheism. Let us confess at once that this conviction cannot be as easily be disposed of as Marx's critique of any proofs of God's existence. Man must choose, says Marx, between Zeus, the enslaver of man, and Prometheus, self-realization; that's why anyone who opts for the gods chooses self-alienation. Marx resolutely opted for Prometheus and he was right, of course. If God does indeed prevent man from being-man, then man has no other choice but to reject God.

The big question, however, is whether Zeus, the enslaver of man, typically represents God. In the eyes of a Jew or a Christian, Zeus is a primitive intraworldly god, jealous of man's aspirations for independence and self-sufficiency, who wishes to keep man in slavery. Both Jew and Christian view God as a supraworldly, transcendent God who gave "the earth to the children of man" with the mandate to "subdue the earth" and who "left man to the council of his own hands." In other words, Jews and Christians also should reject Zeus and side with Prometheus; but they do this precisely in order to execute the task entrusted to them by the transcendent God. They opt for both Prometheus and God, but not for Zeus, and they refuse to believe that the affirmation of a transcendent God prevents them from being authentically human. In their eyes, self-realization is precisely what God demands of them as human beings.

Man's conquest of the earth, even of the entire universe, can never be a challenge to this God. Man's progress does not push God out of the way because God is not a part of the universe. That's why man's will to be integrally and authentically human is not contradicted by his affirmation of this transcendent God. On the contrary, man's attempt to be integrally human is the execution of the very task assigned to him by God.

Turning the tables on Marx, we may even ask ourselves whether his *a priori* rejection of God and his limitation of man's authentic humanity to earthly dimensions doesn't do violence to man's integral humanity. Without any further ado, he dismisses the possibility of any fundamental religious dimension in man: "Religious ideas do not deserve serious consideration." This attitude is unworthy of a serious thinker who wishes to foster man's integral self-realization. For if man has a fundamental orientation to God, then man's integral and authentic humanity demands that he realize himself also in this religious dimension. Today there are Marxists who are beginning to see this point.

Marx appears to have been totally unaware of the God affirmed by authentic Jews and Christians. One who wonders why should pay attention to the way the idea of God functioned—and partly still functions—in the society of man. Marx's "practical philosophy" considered the "practical God" whom he encountered in the society of his time. The only God Marx saw there was the God of a religion which served as an instrument of oppression and an opiate; in other words, a God who prevents man's self-realization. Now, Marx may have been blind to authentic religion, but isn't it true that *what passes for religion* can be such an opiate and oppressive instrument? This is the question we must now consider.

Religion as an Instrument of Oppression

Anyone who is somewhat familiar with history knows that God is often introduced in human affairs to bolster a particular situation deemed desirable by those who make this appeal to God. They wish to confer upon that situation a divine guarantee, identify it with God's will, so that it will be accepted, if not gladly, at least resignedly. They parade as bearers of divine authority who speak in God's name. Now, it is beyond denial that religious leaders far too often either themselves misused religion in this way or allowed others to misuse it as an instrument of power to preserve or produce inhuman conditions. Or else—and this happened more frequently—they too easily identified their own ideas and desires with "God's will" in the sincere conviction that they were right. Let us give a few examples.

In the Old Testament the Israelites sanctioned the extermination of Palestine's native population with an appeal to Yahweh:

Yahweh does not wish us to be contaminated by those who adore false gods. In much the same way our Christian forebears in the U.S.A. used the Bible to sanction the killing of the "heathen" Indians.

Dieu le veut (God wills it) was the battle cry that rallied Christians to the Crusades to reconquer the land of Christ from the Mohammedans and, in the process, to slaughter the Jewish population of Jerusalem. If it is God's will, then we need not sit down and consider whether our action is right or wrong; God's will guarantees that we are right. But was it God who spoke or did some human being rashly act as if he had been present in "God's council" and on his own authority deliver the verdict: "This is God's will"?

Kings used to rule by "the grace of God," their will was "God's will," and this alleged identity was not easily questioned by religious leaders as long as the rulers did not unduly disturb the existing state of affairs, no matter how oppressive this state was for many people. The fact that "God's will" was brought to bear on the problems meant that critique was viewed as a sin against God and opposition as a violation of the divine order. Thus inhuman conditions were not eliminated with all possible dispatch even when they could have been abolished.

Private property became so sacred, so "willed by God," that the horrible exploitation of workers in the nineteenth century found little condemnation among official Church leaders. The atheist Marx's *Manifesto* antedates Pope Leo XIIIth *Rerum novarum*, the first social encyclical, by forty-three years. And even then there were local religious leaders who played down this encyclical for fear of displeasing their bourgeois faithful and diminishing their Church support.

All this is past history, of course, but is it entirely past? Or does it repeat itself even today? Is religion still being used as an instrument of oppression by vested interests? Far less than in the past, because many Christian leaders have finally awakened from their slumbers and demand humanity in the name of the Christian commandment of love. But abuses still occur.

In South Africa Dutch Reformed Christians defend their refusal to give equal rights to the blacks and colored as a theological conclusion from the Bible.

In Angola some Portuguese Catholics counter the demand of local Marxists for a more human situation with the remark that God has to come first and that therefore they cannot yield to atheist demands.

In the U.S.A. there are parents who object to integration by saying that if God had wished the races to mix, he would not have made some people black and others white.

In parts of South America there still are religious leaders who continue to side with the privileged classes against any attempts to introduce a more equitable distribution of wealth. They use their religious power to maintain inhumanity.

There are religious leaders who know that discrimination against any minority is morally wrong, yet fail to take a stand against it for fear of offending or losing part of their congregation.

Did Marx have any opportunity to distinguish the true transcendent God from the pseudo-god who is the emasculated Servant of vested interests? Marx's eyes were wide open to the inhumanity perpetrated in this god's name—so wide that, in his sincere concern for his fellowmen, he became blind to any other aspects of the question and saw only "theological inhumanity." Where thousands of professional ethicists and moralists who believed in God and love of fellowman saw nothing, Marx, the atheist, had a clear vision of the inhumanity "Christendom" inflicted on the oppressed. Fortunately today one need not become an atheist to see the demands of humanity which Marx perceived. That's why today no one is entitled to simply identify religion as such with an instrument in the hands of people who wish to oppress their fellowmen.

What Marx's critique of religion has made evident in this matter is that in the long run an inauthentic appeal to religion in order to absolutize a human situation can effectively ruin man's openness to God. Out of an ill-conceived regard for "sacrosanct" property rights, the official Churches failed to see in time the distinct character of private ownership of social means of production and absolutized the "sacred" character of such property in the same way as ordinary private property which serves the personal needs of a family. Thus, in the name of God or the natural law, they sided with the bourgeoisie and their exploitation of the workers, thereby causing "the scandal of the loss of the working class" to Christianity in some parts of Europe.

As far as Christianity is concerned, the beginning of the Church's stance in favor of the established socio-political structures may be traced to Emperor Constantine's Edict of Milan in 313. In consequence of this Edict, Christianity began to occupy a privileged position in the Roman Empire; it acquired a vested interest in the preservation of the "establishment" and became institutionalized as "Christendom." Thus its leaders became less clear-sighted with respect to the demands imposed by Christianity's Gospel of brotherly love for all. Unlike historians of the past, who viewed the Edict of Milan as a hallmark of Christian achievement, today's more sober-minded scholars tend to see also its disastrous consequences for an authentic and dynamic Christianity.

We owe Marx a debt of gratitude for unmasking the kind of mystification which changed a man-made economic situation of privileges for the few and oppression for the many into a state of affairs guaranteed by God. Unfortunately, the same kind of mystification has re-appeared even more banefully in the political system of official Marxism. God doesn't guarantee anything there, of course, but humanity is guaranteed by the proletariat (which doesn't have any private interests), which is represented by the Party (which doesn't have any private interests), which is represented by a "Troika" or the Party's Secretary (who doesn't have any private interests). Thus the Secretary represents mankind, the fullness of humanity. Woe to him who dares to disagree, criticize or oppose mankind in its representative. He is an enemy of authentic humanity, bent on alienating man from his self-realization.

Man's Coming of Age as a Social Being

There is another point that deserves our attention in connection with the preceding considerations. Marx, we saw, objected to the so-called Christian State, that is, a State which represents God on earth, interprets his will and thus claims a divine guarantee for its laws. Such a view of the State was defended in Marx's time by Julius von Stahl. But Marx argued that politics are a function of man's reason and philosophy and not of religion. Politics, therefore, which appeal to religion are not yet true politics, but a sign that man as a political being has not yet been emancipated; he has not yet come of age.

In a similar way, Marx argues that man's economic situation is the result of human actions. Claiming that such a situation is sanctioned by "sacred rights," that is, divinely imposed laws, is nothing but a religious mystification perpetrated by vested interests. The same applies to man's social relations with his fellowmen; they are man-made, no matter how much some people love to ascribe them to "God's will."

When Marx wishes to remove all religious mystifications from man's economic, social and political activities, he rightly claims that man has come of age in these realms, that he is autonomous in his actions. His activities in these matters are inspired by his project to realize himself in the world together with his fellowmen. How appropriate this project is doesn't depend on man's piety, his religious sincerity, but on his competence in those matters. A believer as such doesn't know more about economics and politics than does a non-believer as such, just as a believer is not *per se* a better swimmer, chess player or poet than is a non-believer.

At the same time it remains true that man's social, economic and political activities can be human or inhuman, foster or prevent the self-realization of his fellowmen. One who wishes to be authentically human must endeavor to humanize his socio-economic and political activities. For a believer in the Judeo-Christian God, the humanization of those activities is a demand imposed upon him by God's will, for God wills that he love his fellowmen. But this doesn't mean that the believer can *therefore* present his concrete proposals as expressions of "God's will," as guaranteed by God. All he can say is this: "God wills that I love my fellowman and that this love effectively find expression in my actions." He cannot add: "Consequently, my concrete actions will, as a matter of fact, help my fellowman to realize himself as a human being." The believer, just as much as the unbeliever, can cause calamities and disasters. The sincerity of his intentions merely guarantees that he will not be subjectively guilty, but in every other respect he is exposed to the danger of failure. History offers us many examples of sincere believers who with the best of intentions made numerous victims.

For one who believes in God, his belief offers no blueprint of the concrete course his activity should take. There are no signs from heaven telling him concretely what he ought to do; nor can he dial heaven to find the answer. He cannot say: "I stand for God and his glory; therefore, I am right." Man is indeed autonomous in his economic, social and political activity. He must act on his own response-ability, his ability to respond to the call for love and respect coming to him from his fellowmen. Belief that this call, in the last resort, comes from God's will may spur the believer to intensify his efforts, but it doesn't in the least improve his ability to guarantee success. And if he thinks the contrary, he is likely to become intolerant of opposition, tyrannical in his behavior and conservative in his views.

Here, again, we owe a debt of gratitude to Marx, who has mightily contributed to the view that religion cannot and should not guarantee socio-economic and political systems. Let us now see about religion as "opium of the people."

Religion as Opium of the People

In Marx's eyes, religion is not only an immobilizing force which tries to stop the course of history, and a tool of oppression in the hands of the privileged classes, but also functions as an opiate preventing people in their wretchedness from remedying their misery. It offers the exploited "consolation" by making them look forward to happiness in the future rather than the present.

What are the "consolations" needed by people who are hungry, thirsty, naked, sick, ill-housed and ignorant? Obviously, food, drink, clothing, medicine, decent housing and education; in other words, "earthly consolations." One who tells them to be concerned only with their "soul," God and the hereafter where "all tears will be wiped away" simply makes a mockery of them. Marx obviously was right when he ridiculed that kind of concern with fellowmen. People are not spirits but embodied beings who need material goods if they are to attain any form of authentic self-realization.

Marx was right again when he insisted that we must introduce into our society structures which will put such earthly goods within the reach of all its members. The availability of such goods cannot be left to the condescending "charity" of the few but should become a "right" for all. Authentic humanity should be embodied in the very framework of society. In the past, relying on a too spiritualistic interpretation of the Gospel, Christianity as an institution often failed miserably in this respect.

But is the "consolation of religion" spoken of by Christianity nothing but a substitute for "earthly consolations" that ought to be present? Is religion nothing but such an imaginary substitute or does it correspond to an authentically human need? The answer to this question depends on the answer one gives to the question whether man has or does not have an orientation to a transcendent, supraworldly God. Is the religious dimension of man an authentic aspect of being-man or is man's existence fully encompassed by the world? Does a transcendent God-for-man exist or not? Marx himself, as we saw, gave no serious attention to this question, but opted at once for atheism. His orthodox followers do the same.

What makes many Marxists particularly angry is that even among the exploited poor there are many who refuse to follow them because of their Marxist atheism. These poor subscribe to Marx's economic social and political intentions, but they refuse to give up the "consolation of religion." Yet, they do not look upon religion as a substitute for the "earthly consolations" which they lack, but as meaningful to them in a different dimension. Marx exhorts us not to pay attention to ideas in the head but to reality. If his followers had heeded this advice and were less pre-occupied with their *idea* of what the proletarians ought to be than with what those people *really* are, they might find here reason to pause and reconsider the statement that religion is nothing but an alienation. Let us add that today there are some Marxists who are beginning to re-examine the possibility of an authentic religious dimension in man.

There is one respect, however, in which one can grant Marx that religion may act as an opiate. Poor people who are oppressed but look forward to happiness in the future are less desperate than others whose sole hope lies in the here and now. That's why they are less inclined to start a revolution; they don't want to jeopardize their chances for a happy hereafter by undue violence. In other words, one cannot count on them in the revolution. Let us recall that for Marx only a violent revolution can bring about the desired state of affairs which will guarantee authentic humanity to all. At the critical moment, however, the believer will become "scrupulous" and thus jeopardize the revolution. He has been "doped" by religion and is unfit to fight.

We may grant Marx all this, but must ask one question: why is the believer in a transcendent God less willing to go all out for the revolution? Not because he isn't interested in improving his miserable situation; he, too, pines for relief from his wretched existence. But he realizes that the revolution itself can be either human or inhuman, show respect for the human dignity of all people or disregard any restraint. He views humanity toward all as God's will for him; that's why he holds that the revolution must not only bring about greater humanity for all but also be accomplished with humanity, that is, with as little violence as possible. He realizes that the desire to bring about a new, more human society does not in itself guarantee the morality of the concrete revolutionary deeds. That's why he shows restraint and cannot be *fully*, unreservedly, counted on for a revolution.

That the revolution itself can be inhuman is rather evident. To bring it about, Marx demanded that the proletariat be made to sink to the utmost misery and was against any gradual improvement of their condition. Where there isn't enough wretchedness to lead to a revolution, orthodox Marxists are willing to cause it for the sake of bringing about a revolution. And after the revolution, dictatorship must be maintained less the fruits of the revolution be lost. A believer in God can still be a revolutionary and a religious leader may even have to become a leader in the revolution, but he can never consent to give priority to the revolution over humanity.

Concluding Remarks

A philosophy doesn't fail because of what it says but because of what it fails to say, because of what it tacitly disregards. Marxism is a great and important philosophy because it has made it possible for man to grasp the world through a central reference point which had never been used before and which threw a surprising light on all kinds of questions. That's why Marx may be called a classical philosopher. But Marxism fails because of the way it absolutizes its central reference point and reduces man to nothing but a being-at-work-in-the-world, for thereby it *a priori* excludes any possibility of a supraworldly orientation of man.

Is atheism an essential feature of Marxism? Does a "theistic Marxism" truncate the very essence of Marxism or can Marxism be "purified" from its atheism? The question is debatable. Historically speaking, Marx's atheism antedated his philosophy; he merely incorporated his atheism into it as a special form of alienation. But the God rejected by Marx is not the God known in Judeo-Christian revelation. Secondly, the antithesis of Marxism as a socio-economic and political system is not theism but liberal capitalism. There simply are no specifically Judeo-Christian economics, politics and sociology guaranteed by God.

Judeo-Christian ethics rightly object, of course, to the disregard for the unique value of the person which underlies the theory of Marx and the practice of Communist countries. And Marxists rightly object to the same disregard which still permeates the practice of so-called Christian countries. Christians can learn much from Marxist concern with "authentic humanism": if Christians take love for fellowmen seriously, they must introduce objective structures in society to make the world really accessible to all. Marx's real objection to religion was precisely that it did not do this.

This point remains important today—especially today. Seventeen per cent of the world's population—North America and Europe—own eighty per cent of the world's wealth. Concretely speaking, this means starvation, disease and generally inhuman conditions of existence for most of our fellowmen. This situation is a man-made condition, it doesn't result from nature's laws but from structures created by man. The fact that we personally did not make this condition doesn't mean that we can wash our hands in innocence, for we live off the system and flourish by it. If we do nothing to change it when we are able to do something, then we consent to it, we approve it and therefore share in the guilt for it. We fall short, grievously short of our professed love for fellowmen. That's the message which Marxism holds out to all believers in the Judeo-Christian God.

There exists an atheistic form of existential phenomenology, in which man is reduced to nothing but a being encompassed by the world. Its proponents, such as Sartre, claim that it is the only kind that deserved to be called existential thinking. But there are also theistic philosopers of existence who reject the arbitrary *a priori* claim of Sartre and demand for themselves the right to begin with man as a being open not only to the world but to any possible reality. May we not assume a similar position with respect to Marx? If we remove his absolutism and his antiquated nineteenth century scientism, we could grant him that man is essentially a worker (but not only a worker), that man's authentic humanity depends on his development of the world (but is not limited to the world), that the economic infrastructure exercises an enormous influence on everything else (without absolutely determining it), that a faulty infrastructure leads to all kinds of alienations and therefore must be changed (although not necessarily by a violent revolution), that the new structures must make self-realization possible for all people (although they cannot guarantee it), and that religion, as it concretely existed, has often adored pseudo-gods (although that was merely pseudo-religion).

Such an "amended" Marxism is no longer orthodox, of course, but it would still preserve the inspiration given by Marx. It would be a view which no believer in God would have to reject on the ground of his faith. And it would provide a working hypothesis on which both Judeo-Christians and Marxists could join hands to make the earth a dwelling-place worthy of man. One would not even need to be a Christian or a Jew to collaborate in this, for these aspects of Judeo-Christian ethics have now become generally accepted by all.

SUGGESTED READINGS

Feuerbach, *The Essence of Christianity*, Harper Torchbooks, 1957. Read also the introductory essay by Karl Barth.

Marx, *Economic and Philosophic Manuscripts of 1844*, Moscow, n.d. All contained in Erich Fromm's *Marx's Concept of Man*, Ungar, New York, 1961.

Writings of the Young Marx on Philosophy and Society, ed. by Loyd D. Easton and Kurt H. Guddat, Anchor Books, 1967.

Marx and Engels, *Manifesto of the Communist Party*, Moscow, n.d. Many editions.

Luijpen, *Phenomenology and Atheism,* Chapter Three.

Koren, *Marx and the Authentic Man,* Duquesne University Press, 1968.

Gajo Petrovic, *Marx in Mid-twentieth Century,* Anchor Books, 1967.

Paul Oestreicher, ed., *The Christian Marxist Dialogue,* Macmillan, 1969.

Giulio Girardi, *Marxism and Christianity,* Macmillan, 1968.

Albert Dondeyne, *Faith and the World,* Duquesne University Press, 2nd impr., 1965.

CHAPTER FOUR

MORAL ATHEISM

1. INTRODUCTION

IN CHAPTER ONE we saw how man's coming of age with respect to nature resulted in the desacralization of the natural world and its spontaneous structures; we also saw how the autonomy of science can be exaggerated and lead to atheism when man claims that only that exists which can be verified by physical science. Chapter Two indicated how a similar exaggeration of psychology's value can reduce God and religion to mere psychical phenomena and lead to the denial of God's existence on the basis of psychologism. Chapter Three examined the desacralization of the established social order, man's coming of age with respect to society. We saw there how making the God of religion the guarantee of the established social order can induce people to reject God entirely.

In the present chapter we will discuss man's coming of age with respect to morality, the desacralization of the moral order. In this respect, too, man's growing maturity did not come about without a religious crisis and a denial of God because God was viewed as the guarantee of the established morality. The man who brought this matter to a crisis was Friedrich Nietzsche (1844-1900).

In his youth Nietzsche was very pious. The son and grandson of Lutheran ministers, he grew up in an atmosphere of Christian religiousness, looking upon God as his heavenly Father and firmly determined to consecrate his life to God's service as a minister. In his late teens he went, as most people do, through a period of serious religious doubts and difficulties, but these had apparently disappeared by the time he graduated from the Gymnasium at the age of twenty.

Going to Bonn to pursue further studies, Nietzsche became acquainted with the then current critique of the Gospels and the critical examination of the sources of the New Testament. David Strauss's LIFE OF JESUS, with its denial of Christ's divinity and revelation, made a profound impression on him. In philosophy and theology he encountered insuperable difficulties with respect to God's relation to man. Medieval thinking about this matter impressed him as nothing but a vilification of the earth and of man; and the infamy of all this reached its apex in the Reformers' scandalous doctrine of man's predestination for eternal happiness or eternal punishment: "Grandiose but barbarian." At the age of twenty-one, when he transferred to Leipzig for further studies, Nietzsche was already an atheist. Writing to a friend, he said that if Christianity is supposed to refer to a historical event and a historical person, he no longer wants to have anything to do with it, but he still granted that it could have some merit to the extent that it was in harmony with Schopenhauer's fundamental ideas.

In 1869, before he had even earned his doctorate, Nietzsche became professor of philosophy at Basel. (This was such an unusual event in Germany that the university of Leipzig gave him his doctorate without a final examination.) He resigned in 1879 and travelled to various places in search of a cure for his shattered health and mental afflictions. Some of his best-known works are THE DAWN OF DAY (against the morality of self-renunciation), GAY WISDOM (against Christianity), THUS SPAKE ZARA-

THUSTRA (about the coming of Superman), BEYOND GOOD AND EVIL (the will to power), A GENEALOGY OF MORALS and WILL TO POWER.

2. NIETZSCHE'S PHILOSOPHY OF MAN AND GOD

Nietzsche's View of Man

One would search in vain for a systematic treatise of philosophy *à la Kant* in Nietzsche's work. His style of thinking and writing is at the opposite pole from that of his famous compatriot. This doesn't mean, however, that Nietzsche's work is a "tale told by an idiot," that it has no rime or reason. With respect to man in particular, his philosophy has its own central reference point, which is the "will to power."

Nietzsche calls upon man to be himself, but selfhood, for Nietzsche, means most of all being-a-body. Man must dare to be a bodily being; he is "body entirely and nothing more and the soul is only a name for something in the body."[1] This sounds rather extreme, but we should recall that Nietzsche lived at a time when exaggerated spiritualism was still very strong. His call to man to be a self, then, should not be understood in a modern personalistic sense, for it is primarily a call to man to be a bodily being. At most one could speak here of a biological personalism.

If man is primarily a bodily being, then there are only two important types of man, viz., the healthy and the sick, the strong and the weak. Both types suffer in life, but the reasons are not the same. The sick and the weak suffer because they are miserable and would like to abolish all suffering and be happy. But it is impossible to do this; that's why the weak take a negative attitude toward life and become increasingly more decadent. Instead of being a self, the weak man is a slave. The

1. *Thus Spake Zarathustra* (hereafter quoted as *Zarathustra*), in *The Philosophy of Nietzsche*, p. 32.

strong man also suffers in life, but his suffering doesn't come from weakness but from a superabundance of life. He knows that greatness and nobility arise only from suffering; that's why he faces life unflinchingly and accepts the challenge to rise to greatness. He says yes to life, he is willing to "live dangerously."

Only the strong man has a right to exist, and this right is based on the fact that he is the hero who says yes to the world, he is willing to rise to greatness by inflicting pain and sorrow on himself and others. Weaklings have no inkling of the "health" required for rising to every greater power. But there is no other way of being faithful to the earth and avoiding unearthly expectations: "Remain true to the earth, and believe not those who speak unto you of superearthly hopes!"[2]

Life is will to power for Nietzsche, but he sees this will to power as animating the whole world. It is at work in chemical processes, in organic life, in the higher forms of conscious life, such as striving for truth and values: "This world is the will to power—and nothing besides." The will to power is the "solution of all your riddles."[3] That's why will to power is the central reference point of Nietzsche's philosophy. As a cosmic primordial will, it appropriates and conquers, exploits and absorbs the weak. Happiness is not the purpose of anything; plants, animals and men are not on the road to happiness but the road to power; they want an "increase of power." Happiness leads to nothing but decadence; only living dangerously, abandoned, despised and distrusted can lead to power.

Man and Superman

The authentic man says yes to the world, and this yes is identical with the will to power. But man has not yet reached the stage of authenticity. People are only "fragments and limbs of

---

2. *Ibid.*, p. 6.
3. *Will to Power*, no. 1067.

human beings," says Nietzsche; this would be unbearable for me "if I were not a seer of what is to come."[4]

The European man—Nietzsche did not look beyond Europe—has sunk ever deeper into a flimsy kind of mediocrity, a Christian existence. His culture is the product of a sick man. He has philosophized from weakness and misery, hoping to find rest, health and salvation. His culture is a culture resulting from the creativity of hunger, poverty and disease rather than the creativity of affluence and power. That's why European culture is decadent and enslaving.[5]

All this is the result of the fact that the European man has renounced the will to power. The new man can arise only when man decides to say yes to the will to power and acts accordingly. "Man is something that is to be surpassed." Man is not a goal but only a bridge linking animal and Superman. The best we can expect of today's man is that he will be the father of Superman.[6]

Nietzsche at first conceived Superman as a superior kind of being, surpassing actual man in power and might as man surpasses the animal. His advent will be terrible to the petty lords and masters who preach humility, surrender and reasonableness. Wickedness, not virtue, is needed to give rise to Superman: "The vilest is necessary for Superman's best."[7] Later, however, Nietzsche looked at Superman as the highest type of the human species. Napoleon, for example, was a Superman. It is not everyone's destiny to be a Superman; only a few can aspire to it. They will lord it over the others, who will be their slaves and tools. The lords will be hard on them but also on themselves; they will be so strong that they don't need virtues. They will be above all morals; no crime will be forbidden to them except the crime of weakness.

---

4. *Zarathustra*, p. 152.
5. *Beyond Good and Evil*, in *The Philosophy of Nietzsche*, pp. 449 f.
6. *Zarathustra*, pp. 6 and 8.
7. *Ibid.*, p. 322.

There is, however, one great obstacle that still prevents the coming of Superman, and this obstacle is man's belief in God.

"God is Dead"

It is by man's yes to the world that he becomes his own lord and master; Nietzsche's struggle for the coming of Superman is a battle against man's negation of the world. Everything that blocks man's yes to the world, therefore, must be annihilated. But the biggest of all obstacles is man's persistent belief in God, especially the God of Christianity. If God exists, Nietzsche holds, man cannot fulfill his vocation, he cannot give rise to Superman, for belief in God stifles man's future. Only Superman can conquer God and restore hope to man. God still has to be conquered, even though he is dead, because people still cling to belief in him. They cling to his shadow: "God is dead, but, man being what he is, there will perhaps continue to be for thousands of years caves in which they will show his shadow. And we, we must overcome also his shadow."[8]

Like other atheists, Nietzsche has a psychological explanation for man's belief in God. Whenever man is overwhelmed by a sudden feeling of power, by anything that deeply affects him, he doesn't dare to look upon himself as the source of that feeling, but attributes it to someone stronger than himself, that is to say, to God. In other words, man's self-doubt gives rise to religion. He sees in himself elements of strength and weakness; the latter he calls "man" and the former "God." Analyzing this concept of God, which expresses man's fear of life, Nietzsche indicates four reasons why God must be rejected.

First of all, moral precepts of every kind are connected with the idea of God. They forbid the strong to develop their power

8. *Die fröhliche Wissenschaft*, Kroner Verlag, Stuttgart, ed. of Nietzsche's *Werke*, p. 126. German works by Nietzsche will be referred to by this edition.

and thus are hostile to life. For Christianity, the holy man is one who pleases God, but all he really is, is "the ideal castrate. . . . Life ends where 'God's Kingdom' begins."[9] God, then, stands in the way of the will to power. That's why Nietzsche calls himself an immoralist. "I deny," he says, "that kind of morality which has become recognized and dominant as morality-in-itself—the morality of decadence, or, to use a cruder term, Christian morality," in which goodness, kindness and charity pass as the highest values. "To demand that everybody become a 'good man,' . . . a 'beautiful soul' would mean castrating mankind."[10]

It is to be noted that the God of morality stands in the way and is the obstacle to the advent of Superman. Belief in this God exercises a paralyzing influence on man's creativity; it clips the wings of the eagle; it makes whatever is crooked straight. The idea that there is a God is evil and full of hatred of man. "If there were gods," Nietzsche exclaims, "how could I endure it to be no God! *Therefore*, there are no gods."[11]

In the second place, the idea of God leads to the equality of all men. "Ye higher men," says the rabble to the strong, "there are no higher men, we are all equal; man is man, before God—we are all equal."[12] The weak and worthless "are glad in their inmost hearts that there is a standard according to which" the strong and noble "are equal to them." That's why "it is among them that the most powerful antagonists of atheism are found,"[13] for they realize that, if God doesn't exist, no one will continue to hold that the weak are equal to the strong.

9. *Götzen-Dämmerung*, p. 105.
10. *Ecce Homo*, in *The Philosophy of Nietzsche*, pp. 926 f.
11. *Zarathustra*, p. 91.
12. *Ibid.*, p. 320.
13. *Beyond Good and Evil*, p. 522.

What does this equalization mean but the deathblow to the will to power? The strong and willfull are told to judge themselves by the standards of the rabble; they must practice the virtues of the weak. The end result of this is a lower type of man, not Superman. Fortunately, the God who sanctions all this "hath died. Ye higher men, this God was your greatest danger. Only since he lay in the grave have ye again arisen. . . . Now only doth the higher man become—master!"[14]

Thirdly, faith in divine Providence robs man of any motive for striving for power and greatness. Belief in Providence means that man doesn't matter; God determines the future; he takes care of us in all our needs. He cures our colds and helps us blow our nose, acts as our messenger and arranges everything for our good. One who believes in a divine Providence can let his hands rest in his lap: God will provide.[15]

Finally, as long as belief in God prevails, neither man nor the earth can be restored to their original "innocence." Yet, if man is to say an unreserved yes to the world and execute his will to power, then nothing should be immoral in itself. There simply are no standards by virtue of which anything is good or bad, meaningful or meaningless in itself: "All things are . . . beyond good and evil; . . . above all things there standeth the heaven . . . of innocence."[16] Morality itself is immoral when it condemns certain actions as evil and calls others good.

Whatever values there are for man and the world, they are man's own creation; value "came not unto them as a voice from heaven" but is man's own doing. Value is whatever comes from

14. *Zarathustra,* p. 320.
15. *Will to Power,* no. 243.
16. *Zarathustra,* p. 183.

power, but what is born from weakness is evil. But belief in God falsified all this; it speaks about another world, an ideal world, and rejects the real world to which man must be faithful. Belief in God lowers man to slavery by despising the original innocence of his creative power. This belief made God a witness to human ugliness, penetrating into the inmost depth of man. Man cannot live under the pitiful prying glance of such a cruel witness: "He even beheld *me*: on such a witness I would have revenge—or not live myself. The God who beheld everything *and also man*: that God had to die! Man cannot *endure* it that such a witness should live."[17]

When the "sovereign individual," the autonomous "supermoral" individual, finally gets "loose from the morality of custom" and "social strait-waistcoats," he becomes a "free man" having his own "standard of value." He then becomes proudly aware of the "extraordinary privilege of responsibility," his "power over himself and over fate." The "sovereign man" calls this consciousness of his own responsibility "his conscience," and by it he is able "to say yes to himself." This "man of the future" will redeem us from the old ideal of slave-morality, from the will to nothingness and nihilism; he will "render the will again free" and "give back to the world its goal and to man his hope," this "conqueror of God and of nothingness."[18]

Nietzsche on Christianity

In Nietzsche's eyes there is no other religion which lowers man to greater depths and slavery than does Christianity. In more primitive times Christianity might have held some attraction, but today it is simply indecent to be a Christian. Priests and theologians, as anyone can see today, are not simply mis-

17. *Ibid.*, pp. 61, 297.

18. *Genealogy of Morals*, in *The Philosophy of Nietzsche*, pp. 670 ff., 716.

taken; they are liars. That's why Christianity must be exploded, and Nietzsche wants to be the one who does it: "I am not a man, I am dynamite."[19]

First of all, Christianity appeals to God in defense of its enslaving morality. It transforms the resentment of the rabble into a doctrine of justice that can be used as a weapon against the healthy and the powerful, imposing restraints on them. Its "herding animal morality"[20] has produced socialism and democracy, thus curtailing the power of the best, the aristocrats among men. Christianity wants one herd and one shepherd, one sheep like every other sheep; it makes unequals equal. But men are *not* equal, says Nietzsche; and he who demands justice to make all men equal kills the will to power. Superman can triumph only if people become ever more unequal.[21]

Secondly, so-called Christian virtues lead only to decadence, for they interfere with the law of selection. To keep the species healthy, one must eliminate the misfits and the weak. But Christianity demands charity and compassion for them. And this it calls love! Man should love what is healthy and wholesome, not what is decadent and weak. So-called Christian love is a crime against authentic life; life itself becomes inevitably "the loser" when Christian morality prevails.[22]

Humility, temperance, self-renunciation are nothing but means to make man withdraw from the world, to prevent him from saying yes to it. What decadence! The very notion of the

---

19. *Ecce Homo*, p. 923.
20. *Beyond Good and Evil*, p. 494.
21. *Götzan-Dämmerung*, p. 172.
22. *Zarathustra*, p. 214; *Ecce Homo*, pp. 932, 942.

"good man" thus came "to mean everything which should be obliterated." Self-destruction is converted into a value. "And all this was believed in as morality! *Ecrasez l' infâme*!"[23]

Thirdly, Christianity is a no to the world, a flight from the real earth. The Christian becomes frozen in an attitude of contemplation of the hereafter, he becomes unfaithful to the earth. The Christian despises the world and he despises even more the body. He acts as if the body were evil, calls hygiene sensuality and looks upon sex as unclean. A Christian can bring children into this world only with a bad conscience. The hereafter, as man's destiny, says Nietzsche, was "invented in order to depreciate the only world that exists—in order to leave no goal, no significance, no task, to our earthly reality." The "immortal soul" was "invented to despise the body, to make it sick and 'holy,' to inspire a terrible levity towards all those things in life which deserve to be treated seriously, questions of nutrition, housing, intellectual diet, care of the sick, cleanliness and weather." But instead of worrying about health, Christianity worries "about salvation of the soul."[24]

Finally, Christianity mistrusts all joy; it throws suspicion on everything beautiful, glorious, proud or rich. Its priests invented sin to prevent everything that would ennoble man; they block science and culture. Christianity can last only because there are people who are weak, misfits who envy the strong, failures in the world, who like to draw down the strong. "No one is free to become a Christian; no one is 'converted' to Christianity; one has to be sick enough for it."[25]

23. *Ecce Homo*, pp. 932 f.
24. *Ibid.*, p. 932.
25. *Umwertung aller Werte*, p. 258.

In sum, the Christian God is a canonization of the "will to nothing, the counter-concept to life—everything harmful, poisonous, slanderous, and all deadly hostility to life, all bound together in one horrible unit."[26] "The Christian concept of God —God as God of the sick, God as [the preying] spider, God as Spirit—is one of the most corrupt ideas that was ever invented on earth."[27]

Nietzsche directed his hatred of Christianity especially toward its priests, for they are the ones whom the strong have not yet been able to overcome. The priests present themselves as champions of the slaves and the weak, they impose their slave ethics upon the strong. To determine the truth, one has merely to turn any theological judgment upside down.[28] But the priests have learned their tricks from the Jewish religion. Born from resentment against classical paganism, Judaism committed its greatest crime when it spawned Christianity.[29] Now, however, Christianity is nearing its end, thanks to Nietzsche. History will be divided into two periods: before and after Nietzsche, the man who unmasked Christian morality.[30] The time is near when the last pope will be "out of service" because there will be no more believers.[31]

The Death of God and the Tragedy of Man

While announcing the future, Nietzsche also devoted some attention to the consequences of the death of God. His prophetic vocation extended to forecasting "the history of the next two

---

26. *Ecce Homo*, p. 932.
27. *Umwertung aller Werte*, p. 258.
28. *Ibid.*, p. 198.
29. *Genealogy of Morals*, pp. 643, 664.
30. *Ecce Homo*, p. 931.
31. *Zarathustra*, p. 286.

centuries" and describing what must necessarily happen: "the advent of nihilism." Such a forecast can be made, he says, because there are hundreds of little signs announcing the future. The whole of Europe's culture has long been writhing in an agony of suspense as in expectation of a catastrophe.[32] God is dead and belief in the Christian God has become unbelievable; this fantastic fact has already begun to cast its shadow over Europe. True, his death means liberation, it brings happiness, relief and the dawn of a new era.[33] Man will be innocent again. But there are also other, more remote consequences.

Most people are unable to grasp all that will follow from God's death; they have no inkling of the collapse of everything that has been built on the belief in God. Because God is dead, man can no longer pray or find rest in infinite confidence; there is no longer any ultimate Truth, ultimate Goodness, ultimate Power. Man is alone at last, but he also has no longer any Friend; he lives forlorn on an icy mountain-top, without a place where he can find rest for his weary heart. Who as yet has the courage to face such an ordeal?[34]

The death of God means, first of all, that no one will still strive for the moral good, for morality is intimately connected with the existence of God. There are naive atheists who think that they can abolish religion and preserve morality. "Naiveté: as if morality could survive when the god who sanctions it is missing!"[35] When God is gone, the man of the future had better prepare himself for the fact that the will to destroy will become just as essential as the will to create.

32. *Will to Power*, Preface, no. 2.
33. *Die fröhliche Wissenschaft*, p. 236.
34. *Ibid.*, pp. 235, 188.
35. *Will to Power*, no. 253.

Secondly, when God is dead, there will be no more striving for the truth. The search for truth, so characteristic of science, has always secretly lived on the basis of religion. The scientist didn't wish to deceive because it was immoral.[36] But when the Eternal Truth is gone, there is no longer any truth in things. Deceit will simply become a part of life; truth will be manipulated.

Thirdly, as long as God existed, man was the crown of creation, even a child of God. But now that God is dead, man will be equal to the animal because there is no longer any will to truth and goodness. Equal to the animal? No, worse; man is a "diseased animal,"[37] for he has let his mental life lead him away from his instincts. Man is a foolish animal, a laughing animal, a weeping animal, the most unhappy of all animals.[38] Nothing of importance would be lost if, like so many other species, this animal too were to vanish from the earth. On the contrary, his disappearance would purify the earth of a "skin disease."[39]

Fourthly, without God, man's life becomes a meaningless martyrdom. The future man will be his own torturer; he needs no God for this. Without God, the world is chaos, a gap between two nothings, without rime or reason. All so-called values are nothing but bait through which life's comedy tries to pro-

36. *Die fröhliche Wissenschaft*, p. 239.
37. *Genealogy of Morals*, p. 746.
38. *Die fröhliche Wissenschaft*, p. 169.
39. *Zarathustra*, p. 143.

long itself in vain. Nihilism will prevail. "Everything deserves to perish." But one doesn't merely contemplate this; one actually puts one's shoulder to the plough; one destroys. The no of the mind is followed up with the no of the deed. Without God, Pascal said, man becomes a monster. Nietzsche agrees: "This prophecy we have fulfilled."[40]

Nietzsche's Personal Suffering from God's Death

God's death caused Nietzsche personally much suffering. In unbearable loneliness, he endured the vision of the future nihilism that would follow God's demise. A famous passage in GAY WISDOM gives dramatic expression to his lonely sufferings. It describes how a fool on a bright day lit a lantern and ran into the square, shouting: "I am looking for God." The atheists standing there had a good laugh and joked: "Did he lose his way? May be, he took a wrong turn somewhere. Perhaps he is trying to hide somewhere. Could he have taken a boat and migrated to another country?" I'll tell you where he is, the madman shouted: "We have killed him—you and I. We are all his murderers." God is dead; "the holiest and mightiest that the world possessed until now has bled to death under our daggers."

His hearers fell silent before his outburst and looked strangely at him. The madman then threw his lantern on the ground, extinguishing its flame. "I have come too soon," he said, "this horrible event is still on its way." The madman then entered several churches there to entone his *requiem eternam deo* (eternal rest to God). Gently led outside and recovering his composure, he could only say: "But what else are those churches now but graves and tombstones of God?"[41]

Man has killed God in order to free himself, but Nietzsche realizes that man has thus set himself free for . . . nothing. Like

---

40. *Will to Power*, nos. 3, 7, 12, 24, 83.

41. *Die fröhliche Wissenschaft*, pp. 140 f.

a cruel ascetic, he wished to make sacrifices. But out of the utmost cruelty to himself, he sacrificed God in order to worship Nothing. True, it has not yet been done: "The mystery of ultimate cruelty has been reserved for the rising generation."[42] Life will then drag on as in a grave:

> I saw great sadness come over mankind. . . .
>
> A doctrine appeared. . . : "All is empty, all is alike, all hath been!"
> In vain was all our labor, poison has our wine become. . . .
> All our fountains have dried up. . . .
> Even for dying we come too weary; now we . . . live on in sepulcres.[43]

But any desire for a prolongation of life is meaningless; since God is dead, man has no longer any purpose or haven:

> Have I still a goal? A haven towards which my sail is set? . . .
> What still remaineth me? A heart weary and flippant; an unstable will; . . . a broken backbone. . . .
> Where is my home? . . . I ask and seek . . . but have not found it.
> O eternal everywhere, O eternal nowhere, O eternal—useless![44]

In the unbearable loneliness of being without God, Nietzsche finally tried to call God back:

> Nay! Thou back!
> With all of thy great tortures! . . .
> Oh come thou back,
> Mine unfamiliar God! My pain!
> My final bliss![45]

---

42. *Beyond Good and Evil*, p. 440.
43. *Zarathustra*, pp. 146 f.
44. *Ibid.*, p. 306.
45. *Ibid.*, pp. 283 f.

Yet, Nietzsche remained convinced that God was irrevocably dead and that his death would plunge mankind into nihilism. In a letter to a friend he wrote in 1885, "My life is now only a wish that all things may be different from the way I understand them and that someone will make my 'truths' incredible."

3. CRITICAL REFLECTIONS

On reading Nietzsche's works, one is continually struck by the evident pride of their author and his utter contempt for anyone who dares to disagree with him. There is none of the humility and self-distrust conveyed by the very term "philosopher" in Nietzsche's self-appreciation. In his autobiography ECCE HOMO one finds chapters entitled, *Why I am so clever* and *Why I write such excellent books*; and he there calls his ZARATHUSTRA "the greatest gift that has ever been bestowed upon" his fellowmen. It is "not only the loftiest book in the world . . . but it is also the deepest book, born of the inmost fullness of truth; an inexhaustible well, into which no pitcher descends without rising again laden with gold and goodness."[46] If one adds to this his intention to "philosophize with a hammer," to be "dynamite" and to change all values into their opposites, it becomes very difficult for his readers to look at Nietzsche with equanimity.

Psychological Explanations

The temptation then arises to dispose of him in a psychological way and to ask what psychological factors made Nietzsche speak as he did. His tragic life, coupled with his undignified raving and ranting, offers a ready opportunity to dismiss him painlessly as a madman. As a matter of fact, this method was already used with respect to him during his life-time. Referring to such critics, Nietzsche says: "I often had the impression that

46. *Ecce Homo*, p. 813.

I was dealing with scoundrels. What alone seems to interest them is not what is said, but that it is I who say it, and how I may have come to say it. . . . In practice, the only reply to them is a kick. They judge *me* so that they do not have to examine my work."[47]

We have already pointed out the unsatisfactory character of such a psychological approach in Chapter Two where we spoke of Sigmund Freud. A purely psychological explanation leaves the entire philosophical issue untouched and exposes the one who indulges in it to a rebuttal with the same weapon. Moreover, if Nietzsche's works are nothing but the ravings of a half-mad genius, it would be difficult to explain the sustained interest of serious thinkers and the more than 15,000 books and articles written about him. In spite of the antagonism and anger which Nietzsche's works provoke in many readers, there is also in them something that attracts and strikes a sympathic chord. Nietzsche "saw" something and helps to make us sensitive to what he has "seen." In this sense he is a "classical" philosopher, that is to say, no one literally takes over what he has said, but his words contains a vision which is relevant to our personal attempts to express the meaning of life and the world.

Within the context of this book, Nietzsche's way of looking at morality is the heart of the matter; it was his view of morality that drove him to the denial of God. He explicitly admits that "fundamentally the only God he has overcome is the God of morality."[48] What is the morality Nietzsche had in mind when he preferred to be an atheist rather than submit to a morality which, he says, is itself "immoral"? He explicitly identifies it as the "slave morality" of Christian religion; and he lists his objections to this Christian religion and morality:

47. *Die Unschuld des Werdens, Nachlass,* 1, p. 383.
48. *Nachlass,* 3, p. 853.

1. Christianity is unearthly; it disembodies man and reduces him to a mere soul, and is interested only in saving this soul.

2. By its notion of Providence Christianity reduces man to inertia; God takes care of us, so that we can let our hands rest in our laps.

3. Christianity imposes a legalistically conceived morality; an external lawgiver issues commandments and forces man to obey by threatening externally imposed penalties.

4. By demanding conformity to universal norms of morality, Christianity disregards that people are people, each one different from the others; thus it prevents me from being myself.

And all this Christianity does in the name of God. That's why Nietzsche rejects not only Christian morality but also the God who sanctions all this. Let us consider each of these points a little more in detail.

Exaggerated Spiritualism

The first point—man's reduction to a mere "soul" and the unearthly character of Christianity—is already familiar to us. It is a reproach that was well-deserved by much of nineteenth century Christianity. "Flight from the world" and "concern with the soul alone" were typical ways of being a Christian in that century. But is such an attitude authentic Christianity or a relic of ancient Greek philosophy? Both Plato and Aristotle did not hesitate to propose aloofness from the everyday world and concern with "contemplation" as the ideal to be pursued by the authentically free man. According to Plato, philosophers become ridiculous if they try to get along in the world; they don't belong there but wish to be free of it, so that they can devote themselves to the soul and truth.[49] And Aristotle echoes these feelings.[50]

49. *Theaetetus*, 176b.
50. *Nic. Ethics*, I, 5.

Through their influence this idea penetrated into Christian thinking. As long as man practically remained incapable of significantly transforming the earth by letting his actions be guided by his theoretical understanding, the idea of non-involvement in worldly concerns and concentration on contemplation could easily maintain itself as a world-view. And it was against the background of this world-view that Christianity formulated its view of man in the past. The Christian answer to the question of life's meaning became, as it were, inextricably intertwined with the Greek ideal of contemplation and non-involvement. One can see this influence, for instance, in the "Christian" idea that a life of contemplation is essentially superior to an active life; in the "Christian" view that heaven consists in the contemplation of the most perfect of all essences—God; and the "Christian" view that life on earth is *nothing but* a preparation for this contemplation. Moreover, the Cartesian split between man and world and between soul and body served to reinforce the old Greek ideal; it led to an exaggerated spiritualism.[51]

By the nineteenth century, however, the progress made by science had already led to man's theoretical guidance of his action on matter. Knowledge was no longer contemplation or theory, but power. Mind (soul) and body had found each other again, for to understand the world, one must handle it, experiment with it, and by understanding it one can better handle it. Thus it stands to reason that the Greek world-view had to collapse. But once a view becomes entrenched, it is very difficult to dislodge, especially if it becomes interwoven with religion. Thus there really was need for someone willing to "philosophize with the hammer"; we owe Nietzsche a debt of gratitude for his contribution to disengaging Christianity from Platonism in this respect.

---

51. Cf. above, pp. 59 f.

Today's authentic Christian does not consider flight from the world and concern with the soul alone the hallmark of Christianity. On the contrary, he is involved in the world and concerned with the whole man, the man who is a conscious subject living in the world, the man who must give meaning to his world, to the earth, his dwelling-place. What Nietzsche condemns in this respect as "Christianity" is also condemned by today's Christians, but they call it a Platonic misinterpretation of Christianity.

God's Providence

Secondly, we must grant Nietzsche that all too often Christians looked at God's Providence in the wrong way: God will provide; God will take care of everything; therefore, I need not concern myself with it. Let us add at once that, as long as man was powerless to change nature in a significant way, as long as man could not envision the enormous range of his own power to modify the earth and take care of his own needs, there was hardly any alternative to this attitude of resignation and trust that ultimately God would make all things work to the good. But this attitude of helplessness and resignation is not the heart of the authentic Christian belief in Providence. As early as the Middle Ages, Thomas Aquinas had already emphasized that "with respect to man, divine Providence consists in this that God has given man the power to provide for himself and his fellowmen."[52] In Nietzsche's nineteenth century it began to be evident how far-reaching man's power could be.

To be an authentic Christian, one must now recall that man is God's image and likeness by sharing in God's creativity—man is called God's image in the scriptural story of *creation*—and continuing God's creation by re-creating the earth. Leaving things to "God's Providence" when man himself can change

52. *S.T.* p. I, q. 92, a. 2.

them concretely means leaving them to "nature," to the uncontrolled interplay of cosmic forces. One who rests his hands in his lap today refuses to recognize the authentically human character of divine Providence with respect to man; he reduces himself to a thing to which something can happen; he falls short of what he ought to be as a Christian. Again, however, the stubbornly lingering attitude of the past, so criticized by Nietzsche, was inspired by the old Greek world-view rather than Christianity itself. And again, we ought to be grateful to Nietzsche for his contribution in stripping Christianity from its Greek embodiment.

There is another point that is connected with the ideal of contemplation and "Christian" resignation to the *status quo.* One who merely contemplates, easily becomes the guardian of the established order; he has a static view of everything: God has fixed the order of the world and assigned a proper place in it to everything. All man can do, then, is study this order with reverence. Peace then typically becomes the tranquillity of the established order. The contemplator is by his very nature a conservative and, when the time demands change, he becomes a reactionary . . . in the name of God.

Legalistic Morality

Let us now see about Nietzsche's objection to the legalistic morality of Christianity. The French Revolution of 1789 began with the slogan Liberty, Equality and Fraternity, but it did not take very long before blood began to flow and disastrous wars engulfed the whole of Europe. In reaction of the excesses of the Revolution and its claim for freedom, there arose a very strong counter-current in favor of authority. Hegel, for instance, claimed that "authentic freedom" is reached only by "obedience to the law and the legal institutions of the State."[53] Simi-

53. *Encyclopedia,* par. 552.

larly, the leading German Lutheran theologian Julius von Stahl argued that obedience to the State was the only way the individual could be certain of doing God's will: an authority above the individual was needed, he said, because man is radically corrupt. Now, the State represents God on earth; that's why obedience to the State guarantees the morality of man's actions. Similar currents of thought also existed in the Christian Churches. In the Catholic Church in particular one can notice a very strong tendency to centralize authority and emphasize obedience to this authority as the hallmark of the believer.

In this way legalism becomes the concept of morality: a person is moral if he is willing to obey the externally imposed law. The good or evil of a human action depends solely on its agreement or disagreement with the law; one must act "according to the rule." At the same time, one has a ready-made criterion to judge others; if their actions deviate from the law, they are evil. And as long as one observes the law, one can say that one's conduct has been moral and claim innocence of any immorality.

When morality is conceived legalistically, moral education can only appeal to fear for the consequences flowing from the failure to observe the law. A moral *ideal* is not needed as a motive to strengthen man against the obstacles he finds on the road to a moral life. Since the law is imposed from without, the law itself has to provide the necessary motive for compliance, and this motive is the threat of penalties for failure to observe the law. A legalistic conception of morality, then, simply demands obedience to externally imposed laws out of fear of penalties.

We must grant Nietzsche that in his time Christian morality was often presented in a strongly legalistic fashion. And we can agree with him that that kind of morality is immoral, that is to say, it disregards the fact that a person is moral only if he is personally moral. One is personally moral when one acts because one sees for oneself that one ought to act in this or that way. Authentic Christian morality may never disregard the person, for the unique and unreplaceable value of each human being is precisely the distinguishing contribution of Judeo-Christian revelation.

But isn't it true, one could object, that for the Christian morality is identified with God's will and therefore something that is externally imposed upon man? It must be granted that the Christian identifies morality with God's will, but this is not simply a matter of obeying an externally imposed divine command. God's commandments do not suddenly drop out of a blue sky but are "written in man's heart"; that is to say, at a given moment of history man "sees" that as a human being he ought to act in this way or not to act in that way. He "sees" that his very humanity demands a particular way of acting with respect to other people; for instance, that he ought not arbitrarily kill his fellowmen. For a believer, who recognizes that man is man because of his God-given intellect and will, this means that what he "sees" expresses what his God-given essence as a human being demands of him; in other words, it expresses what "God's will" is for him.

This demand, however, is not something static but essentially progressive because man can continue to "see" implications of being-human which previously escaped him. Morality, then, is not something externally imposed upon man but flows from within man himself. And authentic Christian morality means that the demands flow from love, that is, the will to recognize and foster one's fellowmen as entitled to self-realization in a world that is meaningful to them as persons.[54]

Nietzsche's critique of "Christian" morality has contributed

54. One should not present matters as if the so-called Ten Commandments were fixed once and for all by God himself. Reading the original text in Exodus 20, one can see there that they appear given to men, not to women. In v.17, the wife is simply enumerated among the husband's possessions, and the same verse also takes slavery for granted. Subsequent greater moral consciousness has permitted man to improve upon the original version.

to removing the exaggerated legalistic approach to morality. Let us now see about his last objection, viz., that Christian morality prevents man from being himself.

Disregard of Man's Individual Uniqueness

This objection is obviously connected with the preceding one. If morality is conceived in a legalistic fashion, it imposes upon the individual the demand to conform with the general law prescribed for all. Again, it must be admitted that very often Christian morality has been proposed as a morality demanding conformity, so that, from the moral standpoint, everyone simply ought to be a perfect carbon-copy of the established pattern. The big question, of course, is whether this is really what authentic Christianity demands. How did this idea of conformity ever get started?

Nietzsche, it will be recalled, scornfully referred to Christianity as "Platonism for the people." When Protagoras proclaimed that "man is the measure of all things," Plato countered this claim by denying that the *individual* man can be the measure or norm. There are immutable ideas or essences, he said, and these are the norms. Individuality means arbitrariness; that's why it should be disregarded in favor of the immutable essences.[55]

Aristotle did not change this position in any substantial way; for him it is the species-essence that counts. Individuality is caused by matter, which, in his view, is almost totally negative. Matter thus puts the individual in opposition to the species; it causes him to fall short of the goodness of the species. The individual is nothing but an imperfect and perishable sample copy of the species.[56]

The Christian thinkers of the Middle Ages recognized, of course, the distinct contribution of Judeo-Christian revelation,

55. *Kratylos*, 386a; *Theaetetus*, 152a.

56. *De anima*, II, 4.

namely, the realization of the unique and irreplaceable value of the individual human being. But they took over many notions from Plato and Aristotle, and among these the relationship between individual and species. Even the greatest of the medieval theologians, Thomas Aquinas, subordinated the individual to the species.[57] Moreover, individuality comes from matter, which is the principle of unintelligibility; hence the individual as individual is not a source of truth; there is no individual truth, but truth lies in the specific essence which is the same in all. That's why the individual must conform with the specific essence; that's why there must be uniformity and why anything individual is arbitrary. Thus Thomas Aquinas substantially continued the same line of thought as Plato and Aristotle. He did not succeed in fully incorporating the unique value of the individual person into his philosophical thought. He shared with them the prejudice that the fixed and immutable essence, reached by contemplation, is all-important.

If we abandon the ancient view of Plato and Aristotle and put man back in the center, then true is that which is true-for-man, and man becomes the norm of everything because it is man who gives everything else its meaning. And the man to be put into the center is not the abstract, universal man, but the only real man, the concrete and individual man who each one of us is. In reference to morality this means that a way of acting is authentically moral if it is moral for me, if I see that I ought to act in this way. Let us develop this a little more in detail.

Am I authentically moral if I simply conform to the way the group says that I ought to act, whether through its social pressure or through the laws established by its bearers of authority? There are three possible attitudes I can take with respect to the established moral norms. I can simply conform, that is, I do

---

57. *Contra gentes*, 3, 59.

not act because of what I see is demanded of me by the fact that I am a person, rather I take the easy way and avoid antagonism and penalties. In Nietzsche's language, I seek "happiness" by avoiding the danger of unpleasantness. But when I simply conform to what everyone else does—or is supposed to do—it is not really *I* who *act*; rather I am "*being acted*" by the impersonal "everyone" (Heidegger); I am not myself, not authentically moral.

Secondly, I can rebel against the established norms of conduct by doing exactly the opposite. I reject conformity, but not because I see that acting differently is demanded of me. I see nothing as yet and therefore express my aspirations for autonomy in a negative way. I am not yet mature and confuse being-myself with being-different-from-the-others. In other words, I have not yet reached the stage where I can give a positive content to being-myself, I am still unable to be authentically a self and authentically moral.

Finally, I can act on the basis of what I personally see that I ought to do. Now, as a person I am something unique and also a source of truth, but this does not mean that I have nothing in common with the others. Where I see that I am like the others, there authentic morality demands that I act like the others, that I conform to the general norm. But what happens if in some respects I am not like the others, different from them? Then authentic morality demands that I remain faithful to *myself*, even if it means that others will disapprove of me and punish me. Any morality that, without any qualifications, requires me to give up what I see in favor of conformity is, in Nietzsche's words, itself immoral. Where I really am unlike the others, morality demands that I give up the "decadence" of conforming and have the courage to "live dangerously." In spite of all the exaggerations and distortions accompanying Nietzsche's ideas, his rejection of a conformistic morality in favor of an authentic morality is valid. I am *moral* only if *I* am moral, and this means that I must act on the basis of *my* conscience, of what *I* see as a moral demand.

Man's Coming of Age with Respect to Morality

Man has come of age in the moral realm, we said. What does this mean? Little children are immature; their parents make them behave in a certain way and thereby establish external patterns of conduct. They do not appeal to understanding; if necessary, they apply force to that part of the anatomy which in little children is a substitute for the seat of understanding. The parents simply impose conformity on them; there is as yet no authentic morality in a child's conduct. But when the little child grows up, he must learn to see for himself why he ought to act in this or that way; otherwise he will remain a child forever and never come morally of age.

Man must see for himself how he ought to act, what is demanded of him by the fact that he is a human being who must realize himself together with other human beings in the world. Neither nature nor society are sacred to him in the forms in which they concretely present themselves; they are not guaranteed by God. The only worldly reality that is "sacred" is man himself, in the sense that man is the center of all meaning, the norm of all value. Everything else in the world must be seen in terms of man, in terms of the contribution it can make to man's self-realization. What this contribution is cannot be determined by a contemplation *à la Plato* of man's essence, for the answer to the question of what man is manifests itself only in a progressive way as history proceeds.

As long as history remained more or less a repetition of the same limited possibilities, as long as there was but little progress and only a static world, it could appear that the moral norms of conduct were fixed once and for all. In such a situation a believer was greatly tempted to conceive these norms as the "eternal" rules of morality willed by God. But when man and his society develop, and especially when this development occurs at an accelerated rate, as is the case in our era, an appeal to "God's will" as laid down in the established moral code is of little use in determining what ought to be done in the many situations resulting from the changing world created by man himself. "God's will" cannot tell us which concrete system of economics man ought to follow, how concretely man ought to organize society, which physiological or psychological interventions in man's being concretely ought to be accepted. Man himself must determine this by a consideration of all the factors involved and by asking himself: what meaning does such a step have for man's self-realization as a human being? God remains silent in such matters; he has left man to "the council of his own hands." And where there is doubt, neither individuals nor religious leaders can dial heaven to find the answer. The proper norms have to come from man himself; he has come of age with respect to morality; he is responsible for himself.

Having morally come of age, however, doesn't at all mean that man can do whatever he fancies. A boy or girl in their early teens will often sigh: "I wish I were grown up; then I could do whatever I like." But anyone who has really grown up knows that being-an-adult cannot be equated with doing what one fancies. One who has really grown up has reached maturity; he realizes that he has responsibility, that he must respond to the call addressed to him by the reality of the situation in which he finds himself and therefore carefully weighs the pros and cons. One who simply drifts along or lets himself be carried away by his biological and psychological substructures is still immature as a human being; he has not yet reached the stage where there can be any authentic morality. For such a person simple conformity may be the only way of securing at least a minimum of morality.

We do not wish to imply, however, that most people can never reach authentic morality and that therefore conformism is what they ought to practice. Nietzsche held such a view, for his authentic morality is clearly an aristocratic morality reserved for the "strong," the forebears of future Superman. With respect to the "rabble," Nietzsche was quite willing to let them have their "slave morality." To be authentically moral in *everything* is likely beyond the reach of most—if not all—human beings, but the same cannot be said in a less absolute sense. For example, most people who grow up in an environment permeated with respect for their fellowmen learn personally to see all kinds of established moral values as values for themselves. They really see that it is morally wrong to exploit other people or to arbitrarily discriminate against certain groups of fellowmen; they also see that sexual intercourse is not a purely biological action. Authentic morality is within their possibilities.

It is important that the preceding critical reflections upon Nietzsche's ideas about morality are correctly understood. They are intended more as an *example* of thinking critically with Nietzsche than as an exhaustive thematic consideration. Instead of the "example" given above, another could have been given in connection with another form of *absolutism* in Nietzsche's thought. For the critique that can and must be exercised on Nietzsche's ideas will always consist in a refusal to go along with his absolutism.

Nietzsche himself also always refused to give in to absolutism, at least when the absolutism of his predecessors was at stake. But because he only wished to "philosophize with the hammer," one could not have expected that Nietzsche would assume a critical attitude toward his own forms of absolutism. If, however, the thinking of our own time and that of the future are to be fruitful, then those who come after Nietzsche must assume such a critical attitude.

But this *critical* thinking with Nietzsche remains a thinking *with* him. And this implies the recognition that Nietzsche's thought was "not concerned with nothing," not "much ado about nothing." And by the same token it also implies the recognition that without Nietzsche our own thinking would not be what it is. Thus it becomes clear that Nietzsche has joined the ranks of the "classical" philosophers. We owe it to Nietzsche that we are able to disagree with him.

SUGGESTED READINGS

Nietzsche, *The Philosophy of Nietzsche*, Modern Library, New York, n.d. Contains *Thus Spake Zarathustra, Beyond Good and Evil, The Genealogy of Morals* and *Ecce Homo.*

The Will to Power, Random House, New York, 1968.

Luijpen, *Phenomenology and Atheism*, Chapter Five, Section 3.

Karl Jaspers, *Nietzsche and Christianity*, Regnery, 1961.

Herman Berger, *Progressive and Conservative Man*, Duquesne University Press, 1971.

CHAPTER FIVE

ANTHROPOLOGICAL ATHEISM

Nietzsche's rejection of the moral God in the name of man's self-development can be viewed as a prelude to the contemporary existentialistic forms of atheism. Like him, they demand that God be rejected because otherwise it will be impossible for man to be authentically himself. Anyone who recognizes God, they hold, cannot do justice to the dignity of man. Although the accent and approach differ most of the time from those of Nietzsche, existentialistic atheists stress that authentic manhood must be equated with atheism. That's why the title of this chapter reads "anthropological atheism"—*anthropos,* man, is the reason for their rejection of God.

Strictly speaking, in all the preceding chapters also man was the reason for the rejection of God. But one or the other aspect of man became the focal point there: man as the pursuer of science, man as a social being, man as a moral being. In existentialistic atheism man as man is emphasized; man is conceived as a subject in the world and, according to the adherents of existentialistic atheism, atheism is of necessity implied in being-a-subject-in-the-world.

After a brief introduction to contemporary existentialism, phenomenology and existential phenomenology, we will consider the reasons why Jean-Paul Sartre and Maurice Merleau-Ponty reject God in the name of man.

1. EXISTENTIALISM, PHENOMENOLOGY AND EXISTENTIAL PHENOMENOLOGY

Soren Kierkegaard (1813-1855) was the founder of existentialism, but he cannot be called a phenomenologist. Edmund Husserl (1859-1938) is considered the father of phenomenology, but he cannot be called an existentialist. In our time, however, these two movements have largely merged and produced the trend of thinking known as existential phenomenology or phenomenological existentialism. Its chief representatives are Martin Heidegger, Merleau-Ponty and Sartre. Let us see how existentialism and phenomenology arose and how they gave rise to the unified movement of existential phenomenology.

Kierkegaard. Kierkegaard's center of interest was man, conceived as a subject in relation to God. Man can be authentically himself only in his relationship to the God who has revealed himself in Christianity; only in this relationship is man truly existence. But for Kierkegaard existence is something wholly original, unique and unrepeatable. By insisting on this radical uniqueness, Kierkegaard made it impossible to say anything about existence that would be applicable to other existences. Thus he deprived his thought of validity for others; he made it in principle "unscientific," incapable of ever reaching the universal level that is implied in all science, in the broad and classical sense of the term "science." All he could reach was "solitary meditation."

Kierkegaard's followers resolutely rejected any attempt to become "scientific," any attempt to speak in terms of a universal theory about man. But we should keep in mind the particular situation in which they found themselves. The two great moments of thought which dominated their time were the philosophy of Hegel and that of positivism. Now, in both these systems the uniqueness of man as a subject was buried under verbiage. Kierkegaard's followers rightly objected to this disregard for the unique and irreplaceable character of man, but their reaction went too far. One can reject the improper identification of being-scientific with either positivism or Hegel without rejecting being-scientific in every sense. Anyone who speaks in universal judgments about man intends to express universal and necessary structures of man; he is by the very fact "scientific." One who says that human existence is unique and irreplaceable makes a universal judgment about man. Thus Kierkegaard's philosophy is self-contradictory in this respect.

Husserl. Edmund Husserl was at the opposite pole from Kierkegaard. Originally a mathematician and a physicist, Husserl was profoundly disturbed by the endless diversity of views in philosophy. Wishing to do away with this confusion, he launched his phenomenology as an attempt to establish "philosophy as a rigorous science," characterized by the universality of its statements. To achieve his goal, Husserl examined the nature of consciousness or knowledge and conceived it as "intentionality," as orientation to that which is not consciousness. One can see here how Husserl's view approaches that of Kierkegaard: for Kierkegaard man is orientation to God; for Husserl man's consciousness is orientation to the other-than-consciousness-itself. There remains, however, a difference of interest. Kierkegaard was mainly interested in theological-anthropological questions, but Husserl emphasized the theoretical problems of knowledge.

The Merger. In Heidegger's BEING AND TIME Kierkegaard's existentialism and Husserl's phenomenology merge into existential phenomenology. Heidegger presents a "scientific" philosophy of man, while avoiding the narrow conception of being-scientific present in positivism and Hegel's idealism. Existentialism thus gives up its antiscientific bias, and phenomenology its narrow interest in epistemological questions to become a philosophy of man. Not all existential thinkers, however, have made this transition. For example, Karl Jaspers and Gabriel Marcel tend to maintain the antiscientific attitude of Kierkegaard.

The main question, then, for existential phenomenology is the age-old question, What is man? To understand its answer, it will be best to see where this answer is situated with respect to the two extreme positions of materialism and spiritualism.

Materialism. There are many types of materialism, but they all agree that man is nothing but a thing among the other things in the world, nothing but a result of cosmic processes and forces. This view contains an extremely valuable truth, viz., that man is whatever he is on the basis of matter. There is no spiritual knowledge without a physiological process, no spiritual love without a sensitive basis, no personal conscience without a biological substructure. That's why, for instance, the biologist can speak about knowledge, love and conscience without making himself look foolish. But legitimate esteem for what the sciences say in these matters degenerates into scientism as soon as the claim is made that, once science has spoken, there is nothing else to say; for instance, as soon as one says that love is nothing but a chemical phenomenon or conscience nothing but a brain-wave.

The materialist who claims that man is nothing but a thing among things disregards the fact that being-man has *meaning* for man and that things do not have any meaning for themselves or for other things. If there were only things, nothing would have any meaning. Only man ascribes meaning, only man says that things "are" and what they "are": he is the original sayer of "is." Things don't create a science, they don't develop a philosophy, not even a materialistic philosophy. Only man does this; there is something in man which makes him transcend mere things in this respect. This "something" is man's subjectivity, his being a subject. Materialism "detotalizes" man by reducing him to nothing but a thing.

Spiritualism. As soon as one realizes the importance of the subject, there is danger that the subject's value will be exaggerated. The subject is something original in the sense that he cannot be totally reduced to the result of material processes. But one can exaggerate this originality by making the subject the *sole* origin of everything; everything else is then reduced to a mere content of the subject's consciousness, a mere creation of his mind. Man is "detotalized" again; he is reduced to nothing but a mind.

Man as "Existence." With materialism existential phenomenology affirms that man is whatever he is on the basis of matter; and with spiritualism it holds that man is a subject. But it avoids the exaggerations of both systems by asserting that man is an "existent" subject. This term *existent* is used in a very special sense: it indicates that man "ec-sists," that is, he puts himself, as it were, outside himself, out there with the reality of the body and the world. In other words, he is a subject who is embodied and in the world; he is not an encapsulated subject, closed upon himself in isolation from the body and the world. The subject is not without the body and the world. The embodied subject and the world involve one another in such a way that one cannot be affirmed without affirming the other. This is what existential phenomenologists wish to express when they say that "man is existence" or the "reciprocal implication of subject and world."

Man as a subject stands open to the world; reversely, the world is not without the subject.

There are atheists among the adherents of existential phenomenology. One of them, Sartre, even thinks that this trend of thought must be defined as *per se* atheistic and that it alone draws the consequences from a consistent atheistic attitude. But other existential phenomenologists are theists; they view the atheistic or "left wing" brand as a deviation, a one-sided development of the movement or hold that its objections to the affirmation of God are really valid only with respect to the affirmation of a pseudo-god. Briefly put, the existentialistic atheists claim that the affirmation of God is impossible if man must be affirmed as man. Now, it should be obvious that man must be affirmed as man. Thus it follows that God cannot be affirmed. Man and God are incompatible.

It stands to reason that in confronting man and God, one can only oppose a particular concept of man to a particular concept of God. What concept of man the representatives of this modern form of atheism hold we will see. But with respect to their ideas of God, one can point out at once that they criticize the God of Judeo-Christian religion or *what they consider to be the Judeo-Christian concept of God.*

Let us see now why Sartre and Merleau-Ponty reject God in the name of man.

2. SARTRE'S ATHEISM

Sartre doesn't keep anyone guessing about the reasons for his atheism. He tells us without any ambiguity that God cannot exist because the freedom which is traditionally ascribed to God really belongs to man.[1] When Descartes speaks about divine freedom, says Sartre, he ascribes to God absolute freedom; God could have made any mathematical truth untrue by

1. Sartre, *Situations*, I, Paris, 1947, pp. 314 f.

merely willing it; whatever is true is true only because God willed it to be true; whatever is good, whatever has any meaning or value is good, has meaning or value only because God willed it to be good, have meaning or value. God created goodness and truth exactly as he freely and autonomously willed it.[2]

But what Descartes really wanted to say, argues Sartre, is that man himself enjoys this autonomous freedom or creativity. Caught in the grip of Platonism with its eternal truths and values, he could not bring himself to say it. While all this leaves the question as to what Descartes meant by human freedom very much where it was before, it makes this much clear: for Sartre freedom means absolute creative autonomy.

Man himself in all freedom assigns meaning to everything. Nothing has any meaning in itself, but everything derives its meaning exclusively from man's free project of himself and his world.[3] Even so-called acts of passion, says Sartre, e.g., a passionate flight to save my life, derive their meaning solely from a free project—in this case my self-chosen project to save my life.[4] We can agree here with Sartre that motives have meaning only in virtue of a project. But Sartre disregards that my project itself is situated in a concrete setting, that a project can be *authentically human* only to the extent that passions and emotions do not remove my freedom. Man is an embodied subject living in a concrete world, and the concrete situation of this subject can make it meaningless to speak of freedom with respect to a particular project. By disregarding that as a subject and giver of meaning I am restricted by my situation, Sartre manages to conceive my being-a-subject as having absolute autonomy and freedom in my project of self-realization. Being absolutely free, I also have absolute responsibility for myself according to Sartre. Man himself is the sole author of his world

2. *Ibid.*, pp. 333 f.
3. Sartre, *Being and Nothingness*, p. 572.
4. *Ibid.*, pp. 443 ff.

and of himself; he carries the weight of the whole world on his shoulders.

Regarding morality, Sartre claims that there are no universal moral norms or values because there is no God who wrote such norms in heaven. This is very annoying, he says, but since there is no God, someone else has to invent values to give meaning to life. And this "someone else" is man himself, for values always presuppose man as the subject. Thus, "it follows that my freedom is the unique foundation of values and that *nothing*, absolutely nothing, justifies me in adopting this or that particular value, this or that particular scale of values."[5]

An immediate consequence of this is that Christian morality offers us no firm foundation to which we can cling as a guarantee.[6] By way of illustration, he refers to the case of a priest whom he met in a prisoners of war camp. This man's father had died when he was still a young boy and had left the family penniless. Being a good student, he had been accepted in a boarding school as a charity case, but failed to receive the scholastic honors due to his achievements because he was only a charity student. When he later fell in love with a girl, again he failed to gain her. Similarly, he miserably failed in his military service. Then, one day, while meditating on all these failures, he suddenly saw these events as signs of God's will calling him to become a priest. Why, says Sartre, did he see those failures as divine signs calling him to the priesthood? Why not as signs telling him to become a carpenter? The only possible reason is that he himself gave these signs the meaning he wished them to have. He didn't want to be a carpenter, but freely decided for the priesthood. He himself remained fully responsible for his option.

5. *Ibid.*, p. 38.
6. Sartre, *Existenialism and Humanism*, p. 47.

Moreover, Sartre continues, even if there were universal norms of morality, they would be useless; they cannot tell me what to do. During World War II, a young man asked Sartre advice: should he stay home to support his aging mother or join the Free French Forces? What does Christian morality say? It recommends love and following the hardest path. But what is love and what is hardest in this case: letting one's mother starve out of love for *la Patrie* or letting *la Patrie* perish out of love for one's mother? What does Kantian morality say? Man must never reduce a fellowman to a mere means. But supporting one's mother can be achieved only by means of abandoning one's fellow-soldiers, and helping these soldiers can be accomplished only by means of abandoning one's mother. It follows, therefore, says Sartre, that universal norms of morality are useless. Even if there were a God who had written such norms in heaven, that would not make any difference. "You are free, therefore, choose—that is to say, invent" your own values.[7]

But, one could object, if man must freely choose his own morality, doesn't this make freedom the universal moral norm? Sartre answers in the affirmative: "One can choose anything, but only on the plane of free commitment." This universal norm of freedom, however, he adds, is not written in heaven but in man himself; it expresses the true meaning of being-man.[8]

At the same time, this universal moral norm of freedom offers a criterion to judge the deeds of others. Anyone who seeks a divine guarantee for his actions in heavenly signs, anyone who excuses his deeds on the plea of passion, renounces his absolute freedom; he lives an inauthentic, immoral life; he is a coward and acts in bad faith. But isn't man free also to choose living in bad faith? No, says Sartre, for then one fails to recognize the *truth* of one's essence, which is freedom as absolute autonomy, one fails to be man. Even in Sartre's view, then,

7. *Ibid.*, pp. 38 f.

8. *Ibid.*, p. 51.

man is morally bound by the objectivity of his essence, but this essence is absolute freedom. A choice which disregards this essence is morally wrong.[9]

In summary, then, for Sartre, man's freedom is absolute. No moral norms are written in heaven because there is no God. The elimination of God makes morality possible.

It is not difficult to see how all kinds of things are confused in Sartre's line of thought. Sartre argues that there are no universal values *in themselves*, that all values are values only in relation to man as a subject. All existential phenomenologists agree with him in this. But it does not follow from this that man is the absolute and unique source of all values. The subject's role with respect to values and norms is to *recognize* what man essentially is. Now, this recognition implies a "having to accept" what man essentially is; it excludes that the subject can be the absolute and autonomous source of norms and values.

God has not written any universal laws in heaven, that is to say, there are no "laws in themselves." We agree, but does it follow that therefore there are no universal moral laws? As we saw above, universal moral laws flow from man's essence, from what at a given moment of history he sees to be demanded as a requirement of his being in the world together with his fellowmen.

No moral system can tell us what we ought to do here and now, says Sartre. We agree again. But does it follow that therefore all moral systems are superfluous? One might as well argue: no general theory of aesthetics can tell me what to paint on this particular wall and how to paint it; therefore, all general theories of aesthetics are superfluous. Or, no general physical theory can tell me what is contained in this particular test tube and how to make the content react with that particular sub-

9. *Ibid.*, pp. 50 ff.

stance; therefore, all general scientific theories are superfluous. A general theory or norm is never designed for such purposes; at most it can supply me with guide-lines that can help me to determine for myself how I should act.

"The Devil and the Good Lord"

The topic that the moral good is God's will is considered extensively by Sartre in his drama THE DEVIL AND THE GOOD LORD. What Christians call the moral good, Sartre holds, is something impossible. No matter how hard we try, man can only do evil. Thus it is meaningless to try to do the moral good as God's will, for there is no moral goodness. Consequently, God's will doesn't exist either. The heaven above man's head is empty; man is alone. God has nothing to do with good and evil.

Goetz, the main character in Sartre's drama, serves as the vehicle of these ideas. One can distinguish three stages in this play: Goetz first tries to do evil and disobey God; God does nothing. Then he tries to do good and obey God; again, God does nothing. Finally, Goetz no longer cares about God and will simply be himself.

In the first stage, Goetz appears as a man who has always done evil for evil's sake and in order to provoke God. Since everything good has already been done by God, Goetz plans something new—evil. He will storm the city of Worms and put its 20,000 inhabitants to the sword to provoke God: "What do I care for mankind? . . . It is God I am deafening. . . . It is God I shall crucify tonight . . . through twenty-thousand men. . . . God knows that. . . . He is afraid. . . . He is saying to himself: 'Perhaps Goetz will not dare.' . . . Weep angels; I shall dare."[10]

The last preparations are made. God does not interfere. "Still no miracle. I'm beginning to believe that God is giving

10. Sartre, *The Devil and the Good Lord*, p. 55.

me a free hand. Thank you, God, . . . for the women violated, the children impaled, the men decapitated. . . . But when it is all over, he will stop his nose and cry that that wasn't at all what he wanted. Do you really not want it Lord? There is still time to prevent me."[11] Goetz wants to do evil for evil's sake, but God, instead of trying to stop him, "does not care a damn."

The second stage begins when Heinrich, the priest, laughs at Goetz's bluff that he does evil for its own sake. What difference does it make whether one does evil for this or for that motive since it is impossible to do anything but evil? "Completely impossible! Love is impossible! Justice is impossible! Why don't you try and love your neighbor? . . . If you want to deserve hell, you need only remain in bed."[12]

This idea is a challenge to Goetz. If no one has ever done good, he will do good. He distributes his lands to poor peasants and, together with them, will establish a kingdom of peace and love. But Nasti, the prophet, predicts disaster. In the new City of the Sun, evil will still prevail. Goetz is obstinate and appeals to the light God has given him. To no avail; Nasti refuses to be convinced: "When God is silent, we can make him say whatever you please."[13]

Evil soon makes its appearance in the City of the Sun. All violence is forbidden, but the happiness of its people drives other landless peasants to despair. Their masters plunder, rape and murder them, but the City of the Sun refuses to put an end to that by aiding the other peasants in their revolt, for violence is evil. Goetz also refuses to assume leadership in the revolt: "God is against this revolt." When the peasants curse him, Goetz withdraws to be alone with God: "Lord, Thou must guide me through the dark night. . . . Let every frustration be for me a

11. *Ibid.*, p. 60.
12. *Ibid.*, p. 62.
13. *Ibid.*, p. 71.

sign, every accident a grace. . . . I must believe that Thou didst permit me to wind up outside the world because Thou didst desire to keep me for Thyself."[14]

At dawn the City of the Sun lies in ruins, burned down by the revolting peasants. When the inhabitants refused to fight side by side with them, the enraged peasants murdered them. But Goetz is not grieved: "Wash your hands of all this blood. We are nothing; . . . Man dreams he can act, but it is God who leads him."[15] He withdraws to the forest, there to annihilate the man in himself: "I am not a man, I am nothing. There is only God. Man is an optical illusion."[16]

Heinrich then visits Goetz in his solitude. He shows Goetz that his so-called "good" intentions were really wicked. Formerly he tortured people by doing evil; later he tortured them by doing good. It is impossible to do God's will: "Torture the weak or martyrize yourself, kiss the lips of a harlot or a leper, die of privations or excesses: God does not give a damn."[17] No heavenly signs tell about God's approval or disapproval.

Goetz now realizes that he has been deceiving himself. The orders which he took to come from God were really self-given. All he ever did was evil, even when he tried to do "God's will." God has nothing to do with good or evil: "I demanded a sign, I sent messages to heaven, no reply. . . . I wondered what I could *be* in the eyes of God. Now I know the answer: nothing. God does not see me, God does not hear me. . . . Silence is God. Absence is God. God is the loneliness of man. There was no one but myself. I alone decided on evil, and I alone invented good. . . . If God exists, man is nothing; if man exists. . . . , Heinrich, I am going to tell you a colossal joke, God doesn't exist. He

14. *Ibid.*, p. 24.
15. *Ibid.*, p. 126.
16. *Ibid.*, p. 132.
17. *Ibid.*, p. 141.

doesn't exist. Joy, tears of joy, Halleluia! . . . No more heaven, no more hell; nothing but earth. . . . God is dead. . . . Alone at last."[18]

And now life can begin anew for Goetz. He will no longer do evil to dare God nor good to obey his will, for God doesn't exist. Good and evil are inseparable on earth. Goetz will now be himself on earth among men, as unafraid of displeasing God as he is not intent on pleasing him. With hell and heaven gone, he is responsible only to himself, in absolute freedom.

A Few Reflections on Sartre's Drama

What exactly does Sartre want to say in the play analyzed above? The answer can be summarized in three points:

1. The "absolute good" is impossible.
2. It is impossible to appeal to God in order to provide human actions with the guarantee of "absolute goodness."
3. Therefore, God does not exist.

After Sartre, Merleau-Ponty and Jeanson also have shown that the "absolute good" is impossible. They managed to do this in such an impressive way that we must dwell somewhat more extensively on this matter.

Objective Sinfulness. If man were an isolated subject, locked up in himself and separated from the world, life as a "beautiful soul" (Hegel), unstained by evil, would be possible. But man lives in the world, in history, among his fellowmen, and this means that the "absolute good" is beyond him.

First of all, man causes evil in the world because he does not perfectly know what he is doing. While *intending* to give meaning and harmony to history, man will *de facto* cause mean-

18. *Ibid.*, pp. 141 ff.

inglessness and disharmony. Man knows what he is doing but, at the same time, he also does not know what he is doing. Oedipus did not wish to murder his father and marry his mother, but he did. The city of Athens did not wish to kill Socrates, but it did. Well-meaning parents do not wish to make life impossible for their children by exaggerated discipline, but many of them do. Parents who abstain from exaggerated discipline do not wish to leave their children without any authoritative guidance and disorientated, but many of them do. The bearers of public authority in a society do not wish to prevent the community's development toward a new future by silencing advocates of progressive ideas, but some of them do. Others who do not muzzle progressives in order to leave room for a new future do not wish to offer opportunities to corrupt the younger generation, but it can happen that they do. Leaders of a church do not wish to irritate its members or make the church ridiculous in the eyes of outsiders, but some of them do.

Secondly, man brings evil into the world because his action also produces side-effects which he rejects and does not approve. One who creates meaning and value within a particular system of meanings must be resigned to the fact that he creates meaninglessness and evil within another system. For example, one who extinguishes a fire on the upper floor of a building cannot prevent the lower floors from being flooded. One who strips backward people of their pseudo-religiousness will make it impossible for many of them to give any structure to their lives. One who does not destroy an enemy having fifty ICBMs when he still has the power to do so must accept the possibility that ten years later he will be confronted with an enemy having five hundred of those missiles.

The question at issue here receives its full importance in the realm of politics. It is ridiculous to object to the "evil" of flooded lower floors because this "evil" is not too serious and can easily be repaired. But in matters political the situation is entirely different. The politician who is not a barbarian will act with an appeal to the ethical ideal. He will have to exercise authority and use force. He intends to defend his fellowmen against "evil" and must be ready to make victims in their defense. And this means that it is always possible to oppose him on the basis of the ethical ideal, for he is making victims. But what does this opposition mean? Those who resist him because he makes victims intend to establish meaning and harmony in history. But when *they* let their intention enter the world to defend their fellowmen against "evil," they must exercise authority and use force. This means that they, too, will make victims, other victims, of course, but nevertheless victims. Obviously, it cannot be denied that they create meaning in history. But the "absolute good" is impossible. In reality, they do not oppose "evil" *tout court*, for they *also* create evil. Man cannot liberate himself from this evil by absolutely abstaining from any violence. For one who renounces all violence in a world in which violence "reigns" makes himself an accomplice of those who profit from the existing violence.

In the realm of politics especially it is true that a meaning which is good in a certain context can be seized by others, placed in a different context and orientated to a future which was precisely not intended by the original giver of meaning. An example is the reproach addressed to Pope Pius XII that he did not protest against the persecution of the Jews by the Nazis. His hands would have been clean, so it is said, if he had fearlessly preached the "principles of justice" in which he believed. But may a man preach justice and disregard the fact that his sermon will produce victims? In Holland Cardinal de Jong did protest the persecution; it did not alleviate the sufferings of the Jews but sent additional victims to the extermination camps. Man sometimes cannot escape a situation in which he has no other choice than to "select" his victims.

From all this it should be evident how reprehensible critics are when they ascribe the objective evil in history to the personal evil intentions of those who have to act and who, even by not acting, act. Politics is not *per se* diabolical and politicians are not *per se* barbarians. But the "absolute good" is impossible.

Thirdly, man's involvement in the objective structures of the economic, social and political world makes a pure conscience impossible as long as these structures *also* embody murder and slavery. Murder and slavery are institutionalized in tyrannical colonial systems, inhuman economic orders as well as the intolerant fanaticism of both pseudo-religiousness and certain forms of atheism. I did not create the world's economic system, in which 17% of mankind owns more than 80% of the world's wealth. I am against the system because it offends my "principles." But this does not mean that my hands are clean, for in a certain sense I "agree" with the system by living off it.

The evil described here is not my personal wickedness. I cannot cleanse myself by withdrawing my hands in order to live with "clean" principles and "good" intentions in the "interiority" of my conscience. One who withdraws his hands leaves everything as it is; he becomes guilty of the personal "sin of omission." His "interior" life is no alibi for the catastrophes of history: there is no pure conscience in a rotten world. The ethical man is a task-in-the-world, a task which is always also a failure.[19]

God "has nothing to do with good and evil." If it is impossible to do the "absolute good," then it is also impossible to guarantee the "absolute goodness" of human actions through an appeal to God. But may we deduce from this, as Sartre does, that God "has nothing to do with good and evil"? There is a

19. Merleau-Ponty, *Humanisme et Terreur*, Paris, 1947, Preface; Francis Jeanson, "Les caractères existenielles de la conduite humaine," *Morale chrétienne et requêtes contemporaines*, Paris, 1954, pp. 182-189.

very special sense—the one presupposed by Sartre—in which it is true that God has nothing to do with good and evil. It is the sense in which Sartre demands that God intervene in the history of evil to prevent evil, just as one can demand that the police intervene in a riot to prevent cars from being damaged. Sartre demands that God offer guarantees in the history of the good, just as one can demand that an insurance company offer guarantees. Next, he points out that one cannot possibly hold that God has anything to do with good or evil *in the above-mentioned sense.* But from this he then concludes that God has nothing to do with good or evil *in any sense.*

Sartre's Arguments Against God's Existence

Sartre has also tried to show explicitly that God must be denied. He offers three arguments to establish his point.

God as the "Supreme Craftsman." God has always been conceived as the creator of man; and man's creation has always been conceived by analogy with the production of a thing by a craftsman. The craftsman first forms an idea of what he wishes to produce; he fixes this object in his mind before he makes it. God, then, is like the supreme craftsman. He knows exactly what he wishes to make; he prefixes the creature in his mind and then makes it exactly as planned. Now, God's creativity covers the whole of man's life; therefore, man's entire life is fixed beforehand. He is nothing but a fixed sample of a fixed species; his life is like the "swelling of a pea in its pod."

Sartre rejects this doctrine because it reduces man to a mere thing. But man is essentially a self-realizing being; he himself gives meaning to his essence as a free being; he makes himself. For Sartre, then, the idea of a creator God cannot be reconciled with the reality of man as a free being. Now, man's reality is beyond dispute; therefore, no reality can correspond to the idea of the Creator God.[20]

God as the "Unstared Stare." To understand Sartre's second argument, it is necessary to know his view about intersubjectivity. According to him, the other subject is always "one who looks at me." As soon as I experience that I am being looked at, I as a subject am reduced to a thing; I am an object in his world. As long as I am a subject, I am the one who gives meaning to the world. For example, if I wish to spy on someone in a hotel room, the door doesn't mean a passage way for me but something which blocks him from seeing me; the dim light in the corridor doesn't mean insufficient lighting but serves to obscure my position; the key-hole doesn't mean a way of opening the door but a possibility to observe without being seen; etc. In other words, everything derives its meaning from my freely chosen project to spy on the man in the room.

But what happens when another subject arrives and begins to look at me? All of a sudden, my project is destroyed; I stop realizing myself as a spy when I feel his eyes resting on me. For him I am bent-over-the-key-hole just as a tree is bent by the wind. Having stopped realizing what I am not yet, my self-realization, I am what I am, just as a mere thing is what it is. He has reduced me to a thing by his look, his stare. Just like a thing, I no longer give meaning to anything; all meanings now depend on him. The dark corner is no longer a hiding place, for he carries a flashlight; the corridor is not an escape avenue, for he blocks it; my mask no longer serves to hide my identity. for he can tear it off; etc. He is the one who gives meaning to everything; my world is no longer mine. I am no longer a subject.

---

20. Sartre, *Existentialism and Humanism*, pp. 26 ff.

And this, says Sartre, is typical of all encounters with other subjects; the other is always the death of my subjectivity: "Hell is other people." There is, however, a way to regain my subjectivity. I am never a thing for other things but only for the other subject. By reducing him to a thing, then, I regain my subjectivity. So, I stare back at him. All relations between subjects, according to Sartre, amount to this: either I reduce him to a thing, or he reduces me to a thing.[21]

Now, God is The Other *par excellence*. He is the all-seeing eye, who looks at all subjects but himself cannot be looked at by anyone. His stare reduces all subjects to things, but no one can stare back at him; he is the "Unstared Stare." To accept God, therefore, is equivalent to accepting that I am nothing but a thing. If man wishes to be a subject, a free self-realizing being, he must therefore reject God. God and man cannot be true at the same time.[22]

God as an Internal Contradiction. Sartre's third argument is more difficult to grasp. It is based on his fundamental distinction between the "in itself" and the "for itself."[23] The "for itself" is consciousness, the being which is for itself and for which other beings are; it is the conscious subject. The subject, we saw, always tries to realize himself, to be what he is not; hence he is negative. Moreover, consciousness always refers to something else of which it is conscious; hence it is not self-sufficient. Consciousness always searches for reason or ground; it is dependent. Exactly the opposite of all this, Sartre holds, applies to the "in itself," the material thing. The "in itself" just is what

---

21. Sartre, *Being and Nothingness*, pp. 257 ff.

22. *Ibid.*, pp. 266, 493.

23. For a more complete explanation of this distinction see Luijpen, *Existential Phenomenology*, rev. ed., Pittsburgh, 1969, pp. 72 ff. or Luijpen and Koren, *A First Introduction to Existential Phenomenology*, Pittsburgh, 1969, pp. 43 ff.

it is; hence it is full positivity; it does not refer to anything else; therefore, it is self-sufficient; it seeks no ground; therefore it is groundless.

Now, argues Sartre, the God spoken of by religion obviously is supposed to be an "in itself," for he is conceived as full positivity, total self-sufficiency, perfect independence. But, on the other hand, this God is also conceived as consciousness or "for itself." In other words, the idea of God is a contradiction in terms: God would be full positivity and pure negativity, complete self-sufficiency and sheer insufficiency, total independence and utter dependence.[24]

Critical Remarks

Sartre's argument against the Creator God would be valid if the creative action of God could be adequately described by way of analogy with the creativity of a craftsman. The maker of a thing "fixes" it in such a way that the thing "itself" is fully determined. But there is also a different type of causality, one which does not take away the subject's freedom, viz., the creative causality of love. Love wills the other subject as a free self-realizing being, it makes the beloved *be* something which otherwise would have been completely beyond his reach. As most young people have experienced, they and their world are completely transformed, they begin to *be* in a different way when their beloved tells them: "I love you, too, Johnny." Yet, the making-be of love does not in any way destroy the beloved's freedom; on the contrary, love is essentially respect for the other's freedom. The causality of love, however, is unknown to Sartre. This is not surprising, for according to him the only possible relationship between free subjects is that of hatred.

At the same time, we must grant that Sartre's critique has rendered a good service to philosophers and theologians who

---

24. Sartre, *Being and Nothingness*, pp. 90 ff.

speak of God's creativity. In the past this creativity was all too often illustrated by examples drawn from the analogy of a craftsman. The creativity of love simply did not figure in the study of creativity and causality.

The same flaw fatally affects also Sartre's *second argument.* If the relationship between subjects is of necessity a relationship of hatred, my experience of being in the presence of another subject would be a feeling of being a mere object in the other's eyes. Then I can remain a subject only by reducing the other to a thing, by staring back at him. As an analysis of hatred, Sartre's description is excellent. But his generalization that all "looks" are stares of hatred goes against my experience. Others can also look at me with a look of love, benevolence, mercy, pity, etc. God as a subject, therefore, need not be conceived as the "Unstared Stare," but can also be a God of love.

Again, however, we must grant Sartre that very often the "all-seeing eye" of God was presented as that of a "celestial policeman" rather than a loving Father. "Big Brother is watching you," ready to pounce on you—that was all too often the interpretation given to God's presence with man. If we couple this misinterpretation with the identification of "God's will" with the norms of conduct established by the group, one can see why God could appear as the "Unstared Stare" preventing man from being himself.

In his *third argument* Sartre all of a sudden abandons the phenomenological attitude by virtue of which he was able to conceive the subject as a project of self-realization in the world. Subject and world imply each other, says phenomenology. This means that I cannot speak about the subject without including the world in my considerations, but also that it is meaningless to speak about the world without the subject. I cannot say what the world or anything in the world is divorced from the subject, in itself. All I can do is indicate what it is for me, for us. Sartre's description of the so-called "in itself," the material thing, purports to tell us what this thing is divorced from the subject. The "in itself"-for-me certainly does not appear as full positivity, total self-sufficiency, independence and being without any ground. From a phenomenological standpoint, Sartre's attempt to speak about the "in itself," about reality divorced from the subject, is a contradiction.

Moreover, for Sartre the "for itself" or consciousness is essentially negative. It, therefore, cannot be the highest mode of being. But when religion ascribes consciousness to God, it wishes to "affirm" of him the highest level of being conceivable to man. For religion God is not a "for itself" in the Sartrian sense of the term. Besides, religion does not ascribe to God the kind of consciousness proper to man. Man's consciousness is "intentional," orientation to the other than itself. This gift raises him above mere things; it ennobles him. But at the same time it implies something less perfect, viz., man's dependence on the other-than-himself. In ascribing consciousness to God, religion wishes to "affirm" of him this nobility of being without, however, also attributing to him the defective way consciousness exists in man.

The Believer in God as the "Grave Man"

According to Sartre, anyone who believes in God is a "grave man." The grave man is a coward because he does not dare to recognize his own absolute freedom, but views himself as if he were nothing but a thing in the midst of things. The grave man is in "bad faith" because he refuses to face his own freedom. What Sartre means by all this becomes clear when he adds that anyone who tries to be sincere is in bad faith. The attempt to be sincere is an effort to be for oneself what one *is* and nothing else. Being what one *is*—that's precisely the definition of a thing. A thing, says Sartre, always simply is what it is; man as a subject, however, is not what he is but is what he *is not*. The subject always goes beyond what he already is and tries to realize what he is not yet. The sincere man resigns himself to being what he is; that's why he is in "bad faith."[25]

The grave man, then, is in bad faith because he ascribes to himself the being of a thing. And, says Sartre, this is exactly what is done by the man who believes in God. Let us see what this means. When Sartre points out that man as a subject is characterized by "negativity," he wishes to stress that nothing man has already achieved can permanently satisfy him. As soon as he has become something which he was not yet, man experiences emptiness and wishes to achieve something else again, he wishes to realize some other potential contained in his being. All fullness is permeated with emptiness, all rest, peace and happiness with unrest, trouble and unhappiness; there is nothing at all in the world that can ever fulfill man. If a man disregards this "negativity" of his manhood, if he definitively says yes to the world, to anything in the world, he commits an injustice to his manhood; consequently, he is in "bad faith."

This is what the grave man does, according to Sartre. That's why he is insincere, a mere "subman" (Simone de Beauvoir). And the man who believes in God is a grave man, he is one who renounces his manhood in favor of the world.[26] The God, then, rejected by Sartre, is a god who is a *worldly* reality to which man gives an unreserved consent. Simone de Beauvoir, who is Sartre's most slavish follower, gives examples of the "gravity" of belief in God which Sartre despises so much: the military man for whom the Army is everything; the colonist who sacrifices the natives to the building of the Road; the revolutionary who is blind to everything but the Revolution—all these are grave men because they are servants of "divinities."

---

25. *Ibid.*, p. 580.
26. *Ibid.*, p. 580.

It is hardly necessary to add that any such "worldly realities" are not what is meant by God in Judeo-Christian religion. Anyone who absolutizes such a worldly reality is a believer in an idol; in Judeo-Christian language his so-called "belief" in God is a sin of idolatry. For authentic Judeo-Christian believers God is supraworldly or transcendent; hence such believers cannot be accused of "gravity," of giving an absolute consent to a worldly reality.

Sartre's philosophy makes it clear that man can never come fully to rest in the world; he can never definitively consent to anything in the world. On the other hand, Sartre limits man to the world and excludes any orientation to the Transcendent. The result of this is that, for Sartre, man cannot give any ultimate meaning to life; man is nothing but a "useless suffering." Having demanded absolute freedom *from* God for man, Sartre's philosophy comes to the disconsolate conclusion that man now has also nothing worth-while left to be free *for*.

3. THE ATHEISM OF MERLEAU-PONTY

There is a strong tendency among theists, complains Merleau-Ponty, to classify philosophies as either theistic or atheistic. With respect to the latter, they then either consider them irrelevant or they try to show that the atheistic philosopher who reject the authentic notion of God as the Absolute and Necessary Being simply re-introduces a pseudo-god in the form of some other Absolute; in other words, the atheist is merely mistaken about who God is. Merleau-Ponty realizes that there are atheists who make that kind of mistake, but he refuses to call them philosophers; in his eyes they are "inverted theologians." On the other hand, he also refuses to admit that philosophy should be defined in terms of the negation of God; one who does this, he says, begins by disregarding what philosophy really is.[27]

---

27. Merleau-Ponty, *In Praise of Philosophy*, pp. 42 ff.

Positively considered, Merleau-Ponty argues, "to philosophize is to seek, and this is to imply that there are things to see and to say."[28] And there is something to see and to say because of man, the subject, through whom there is meaning in the form of truth and value. There is meaning because subjectivity has emerged in the cosmos. Meaning exists only through the dialogue of the subject with the world; there is no meaning in a world divorced from the subject, nor in an isolated consciousness locked up in itself. The little term "is," by which I affirm the world, has meaning only because and to the extent that the subject does not seek any absolute "in itself" or "for itself."

The marvel that subjectivity has emerged in the cosmos makes truth and value possible, but how are we to explain the emergence of this marvel? This question, says Merleau-Ponty, is meaningless; any answer to it is pure nonsense. Explanations are made in the sciences; there we try to reduce things to their antecedents, to the processes and forces which caused it. Explanations, then, belong to the realm governed by deterministic influences, the realm of necessity.

Man as a subject, however, can never be explained. For any explanation conveys a meaning, and every meaning *presupposes* the subject. Man as a subject could be explained if he were a mere thing; he would then be necessitated by processes and forces. But man is not a necessitated thing; man is a contingent being, a free being.[29]

Philosophy, then, as Merleau-Ponty sees it, affirms the contingent freedom of man as a subject in the world. This contingency makes man transcend the thinglike and processlike necessity of the cosmos. As a subject, as a contingent, free source of meaning, man is not "guaranteed" by necessity as things are. His life is not a process but *history*, a search for truth and value or more generally, meaning. He can make progress in this search, but no divine decree or fate underwrites its

28. *Ibid.*, p. 41.

29. Merleau-Ponty, *Phenomenology of Perception*, pp. IX, 170.

success. Some people get "dizzy" when they come face to face with this utterly contingent aspect of manhood, but "philosophy is not a hospital." One who cannot stand it may seek an escape by taking refuge in a history guaranteed by Marxist principles or the Necessary Being of Christian religion. But then he refuses to acknowledge that he is a man; he reduces himself to a thing and a process.[30]

Why Merleau-Ponty Rejects God

The philosopher, then, according to Merleau-Ponty, tries to express the wonder of wonders, the existence of meaning through the emergence of subjectivity. He refuses to explain the subject who is the source of meaning because explanations apply only to the realm of things governed by necessity. And this is why the philosopher must also deny God. For the God spoken of by theologians is the Necessary Being who causes man, the contingent being. Now, such a necessary cause would reduce the contingent or free being to a being-necessitated. In the name of man's contingency as a subject, then, we must reject the affirmation of God.[31]

Merleau-Ponty realizes that Christianity demands the rejection of all idols, that the Christian must be an "atheist" with respect to any god who, as we have explained in the preceding chapters, is nothing but a guarantee of nature, who sanctions all good and evil in the world, who justifies slavery, injustice and the agony of the innocent; briefly put, Merleau-Ponty recognizes that a Christian must reject a god who is the "absurd Emperor of the World." But, in his view, Christianity is inconsistent because anyone who makes God the Necessary Being and Cause of man *by that very fact* also makes God the "absurd Emperor of the World."[32]

---

30. Merleau-Ponty, *Signs*, pp. 239 ff.
31. Merleau-Ponty, *In Praise of Philosophy*, pp. 45 ff.
32. *Ibid.*, p. 47.

Merleau-Ponty and Christianity. Merleau-Ponty doesn't begin his philosophy with the rejection of God, but almost reluctantly comes to the conclusion that God and the recognition of man as contingent freedom are incompatible. Unlike Sartre with his passionate atheism, Merleau-Ponty refuses to call himself an atheist and he does it only under extreme provocation. He "understands" Christianity but does not "accept" it—like Socrates who understood the religion of the Athenians but did not accept it; on the contrary, he rejected it. The marvel of the emergence of meaning through the subject, Merleau-Ponty holds, is talked out of existence by those who accept the Necessary Being.[33] Developing this idea further with respect to the search for truth and the creation of values, he indicates why the Christian cannot authentically participate in man's historical search for truth and value.

Christianity, he claims, is essentially ambiguous. He knows, of course, that individual Christians have often intensely participated in the search for truth and values; they stood on the side of man. Other Christians did just the opposite; they were people who already "knew the answers" and gave them a divine guarantee: "We stand for God." As long as one remains merely on the level of *facts*, a Christian can always disavow the past as something that should not have happened. The ambiguity of Christian deeds always leaves an escape hatch open where one can take refuge in a "heaven of principles."[34]

But the same ambiguity, argues Merleau-Ponty, permeates the very *essence* of Christianity. Popularly expressed, his idea is that Christianity makes its believers live as people who have "one foot in heaven" and "one foot on earth." Pinpointing this fundamental ambiguity, Merleau-Ponty says that it lies in the

33. *Ibid.*, pp. 45 ff.

34. Merleau-Ponty, *Sense and Nonsense*, pp. 172 ff.

simultaneous belief in the "religion of the Father" and the "religion of the Son." The religion of the Father is that of the internal God, who dwells in man's inner self. Man finds him by turning away from the world and listening to God's testimony about himself in one's heart. Faith in this internal God has a dimension of eternity.

That's why from the standpoint of this faith the temporal order is unimportant. Man's temporal actions, whether they be good or evil, can add or subtract nothing with respect to the infinite, eternal goodness of God: "Good resides only in the spirit, and finally in God, who is eternal"; therefore, on this side of the world, "there is, strictly speaking, nothing to do."[35] Man's fate on earth no longer matters in the light of the internal God; he merely has to say, "Thy will be done." Human history, man's search for truth and value, becomes irrelevant before such faith in the "reign of the Father."

But Christianity is also belief in the religion of the Son. When God became incarnate in Christ, faith in an "external God" came into existence: God is no longer found in man's heart but in the exteriority of history; God has lived at a particular time and place, giving signs and leaving behind his words. Now man can no longer withdraw from the world; he must involve himself in it, he must grapple with good and evil.[36]

The paradox and ambiguity of Christianity, according to Merleau-Ponty, lie precisely in this that the Christian "never clings either to the internal God or to the external God, but always takes a position that lies *in between* those two possibilities." One can see this in all kinds of ways. The Christian is ready to lose his life, for he knows that by losing it he will gain it. The Christian calls faith a leap in the dark, but he knows where he will land. His religion calls for surrender, but he knows to whom he entrusts himself. He accepts that history is

35. *Ibid.*, p. 174.
36. *Ibid.*, pp. 174 ff.

important but, at the same time, it is also unimportant for him since the wisdom of the Father has already settled everything; why, then, shouldn't he who knows all this use force against his fellowmen when they are merely wasting time in their ceaseless searching and groping for truth and value?[37]

This fundamental ambiguity of the Christian makes him unreliable in practical political matters. One can never fully count on him. His belief in the religion of the Son makes him a revolutionary, but his belief in the religion of the Father makes him a conservative. But in both capacities, as revolutionary or as conservative, the Christian is unreliable. When decisions are to be made in the revolution, the Christian will shy away from progress with the plea that evil is forbidden. At the same time, he is a nuisance to the establishment, for he is likely to remember that the religion of the Son means participation in the making of history and fostering man's progress; hence the conservatives cannot count on him either; he may join the revolution after all.[38]

The Catholic Church in particular suffers from this unreliability and doesn't even seem to *really* believe in the Incarnation. It allows revolution in one case, viz., when authorities violate the divine law. In actual fact, however, this Church has never sided against lawful authorities *because* they acted unjustly, nor has it ever sided with a revolution *because* it was just. It only sides with revolutionaries who protect its temples, priests and properties. But the Catholic Church will only fully recognize that God has become incarnate on earth when it shows the same concern for ordinary people as for its ministers, when it protests as much against the destruction of people's houses as that of its temples. As long as it doesn't do this, it demands that its followers practice heroism in its favor and remains essentially a conservative force.[39]

---

37. *Ibid.*, pp. 176 ff.
38. *Ibid.*, pp. 177 f.
39. *Ibid.*, p. 178.

In summary, then, a Christian cannot really be a man; he cannot enter into dialogue with his fellowmen in their search for truth and value, for he is "one who knows" and possesses divine guarantees for his values. He can never be fully counted upon on earth because he has "one foot in heaven."

Critical Reflections

The first two points that need to be considered with respect to Merleau-Ponty's rejection of God are the ideas of causality and contingency. If the contingent subject is caused by God, the Necessary Being, he argues, then the contingent subject is no longer contingent but necessitated. What kind of causality cannot be reconciled with "contingency" because it necessitates? The answer is the deterministic influence or causality which a thing exercises on another thing, the causality manifesting itself in a cosmic process. If the Necessary Being causes the contingent subject just as a cosmic force causes a thing, then Merleau-Ponty is right. Any philosophical or theological argument which makes God's causality with respect to the contingent subject similar to a natural process resulting in a thing destroys this subject and reduces him to a mere thing.

But is this the only possible way one can look at causality, the only possible way of exercising influence, of "making be"? We already touched this question in connection with Sartre's rejection of the Creator God, where we pointed to the creative causality of love. Love is an intersubjective relationship in which one fosters and develops the other subject while respecting his freedom. Children who do not experience sufficient love in their early years fail to develop into integral subjects, capable of authentic person-to-person relations with others. Having been reduced to mere things or functions in their tender years, they tend to treat other subjects as things or functions; they don't know what it means to be together subject to subject. Love, on the other hand, transforms a subject and his world. When a girl understands that her boy-friend really loves her and wishes to marry her, she becomes transformed: a new world goes open to her, a world in which she is no longer "alone"; she can give to herself and her world a fuller meaning, thanks to the other's love.

Love, then, re-creates the beloved, makes him or her be more fully a subject; at the same time, it re-creates the beloved's world. Yet, love does not force; the very idea of forcing is foreign to love. Love can be fruitful or creative only if it is freely accepted and respects the beloved's freedom. Now, if God's creative causality with respect to the contingent subject who man is, is conceived as a causality of love, then Merleau-Ponty's objection loses its sting; God's causality does not stifle or destroy man's subjectivity. It is significant that the consideration of love is lacking in Merleau-Ponty's philosophy. But let us not forget that theologians and philosophers in the past also used to neglect the creative causality of love when they spoke of God as the cause of all beings. Their illustrations of causality were taken from the realm of things.

Regarding contingency, paradoxical as it seems, traditional metaphysics has always affirmed the existence of the Necessary Being on the basis of contingency, while Merleau-Ponty is led to reject God on the basis of contingency. This arouses at once the suspicion that the meaning which "contingency" has for him is not the same as its meaning in traditional metaphysics.

For Merleau-Ponty the term "contingency" has an anthropological meaning. It expresses the mode of being proper to the subject, it indicates that the subject is not necessitated, the result of deterministic causes, a mere thing. To be contingent means to be free. Only the subject is contingent. For traditional metaphysics, on the other hand, "contingency" has an entirely different meaning. A being is contingent if it does not have a sufficient reason for its being within itself. In this sense, then, not only subjects but also things are contingent.

The question raised by the metaphysician is not the same as that raised by Merleau-Ponty. One must even say that he is a total stranger to the metaphysical question. That's also the reason why he rejects all metaphysical "explanations." "To explain" has only one meaning for him, viz., to see a thing is relation to its deterministic antecedents. Thus, his statement that theology is unable to explain the subject's contingency with respect to God means that the subject's freedom cannot simply be the result of a thinglike process. *If* one accepts Merleau-Ponty's sense of the terms "contingency" and "causality," his assertion is true, of course. In this sense he cannot be "refuted." But one can add that his consideration of the subject is too narrow because it disregards the metaphysical dimension of man. Merleau-Ponty is so preoccupied with the search for the dark roots of human rationality in the "body-subject" that he never comes to grip with the dilemma faced by the metaphysician: either there is nothing at all or there is an all-explanatory principle.

Merleau-Ponty's Critique of Christianity

Regarding Merleau-Ponty's critique of Christianity, what he really wishes to say can be summarized in the assertion that Christian believers in God cannot take the world and its history seriously. Possessing God, who is Truth itself, they "know" the truth and need not participate in the "dizzy" search for it; possessing the God who is Goodness itself, they need not become involved in the dangerous enterprise of establishing values. From the standpoint of the search for truth, they are intolerant, and in the struggle for a more human world they are conservative. Although God's entrance into human history through the Incarnation has changed all this to a certain extent, Christianity remains essentially ambiguous. Because they have one foot in heaven, Christians need not do anything, for everything will be all right.

Let us begin by pointing out that the early Christians would have been very much surprised if anyone had told them that there was nothing left for them to do now that they had become Christians. In their eyes, everything had just now begun again; the world had received a new meaning and this meaning offered them motives to go to work in order to make this new meaning effective. With this conviction they set to work and succeeded in giving a new meaning to the world through their effective love of fellowmen.

Yet, Merleau-Ponty is right when he argues that there is a certain ambiguity in Christianity. Bipolarity is a distinguishing characteristic of the Christian; he is orientated both to God and to the world in his project of existence, and this bipolarity influences his conduct. Now, for one who rejects God the Christian's orientation to God will appear at once as an alienation, for the atheist recognizes only man's orientation to the world. For the Christian himself his bipolarity means that he will always live in a situation of tension between world and God; he has to realize himself according to both. The task of doing this is never ended but presents itself in ever new forms. No past solution will appear satisfactory when the situation changes. One cannot count on it that a Christian will always offer the same answers. He is a bad revolutionary and a bad conservative.

For Merleau-Ponty the Christian's essential ambiguity arises from his orientation to God. He would be fully human only if he were to abandon this orientation and describe himself as *nothing but* a being involved in the world, in other words, only by ceasing to be a Christian would he be able to be fully human. We have here an echo of Feuerbach's aim: let us "change Christians into whole men." The Christian, however, will reject this dilemma; in his eyes, being a whole man implies precisely also recognition of man's orientation to God. And that's why, as a matter of principle, he refuses to buy progress in history at the price of crimes; no revolutionary can fully count on him.

But the authentic Christian doesn't conclude from his orientation to God that, as a matter of principle, he is *not* involved in the world; he doesn't consider himself as *nothing but* an orientation to God. On the contrary, he holds that his orientation to God must manifest itself in his orientation to the world. Expressed in more religious terms, his love for God must shine forth in his love for man.

In *theory*, then, the Christian must be fully involved in the world and its history. As a Christian, he is essentially a humanist, a man who wishes to humanize the world, but he is not *nothing but* a humanist, for he also wishes to realize his orientation to God. These two orientations, to the world and to God, however, constitute a dialectical unity for him, they imply each other. Disregarding either the one or the other is, in the eyes of the Christian, an alienation from what he ought to be.

Is there any guarantee that the Christian will not, *as a matter of fact*, become alienated from either the one or the other orientation and seek the essence of Christianity either exclusively in the world or exclusively in God? Being-man, we saw, is a task to be accomplished, but a task of a contingent, free subject. Precisely because man is contingent, there is no guarantee that he will execute this task as he ought to. That's why he must always be ready to subject himself to criticism, to evaluate what he is doing. Now criticism and evaluation can only be made in the light of principles. If I have no idea at all about aesthetics, I cannot possibly criticize a work of art; I have nothing to guide me in my evaluation. The Christian way of living, therefore, must be examined in the light of principles. Otherwise there isn't even any possibility of saying that the Christian's life is an alienation.

The big question, of course, is which principles? One who with Merleau-Ponty accepts that orientation to God is *per se* an alienation will see all kinds of Christian attitudes as expressions of alienation; for instance, "Thy will be done," "It is not possible to serve two masters," "My kingdom is not of this world," "One must lose his life to gain it." Such attitudes express for him that the Christian is not at home in the world. But for the authentic Christian these attitudes are merely expressions of the bipolarity of his existence; "God's will," for example, does not paralyze his efforts to humanize the world. On the contrary, God's will is for him precisely the reason why he wants to re-create and humanize it. And although God's kingdom is not *of* this world, it is a kingdom that must be brought about *in* this world; it is not a kingdom that all of a sudden begins *after* this world.

If there is a tension between the two poles of being-a-Christian, it is to be expected that Christians will often fall short of what they ought to be. History is only too full of examples showing this, not only in the lives of individual Christians but also in that of Christian groups or Churches. The very core of Christianity—love of God manifesting itself in love of man—can be disregarded. When this happens is it surprising that thoughtful people turn away in disgust, seeing all the injustices and forms of oppression perpetrated in the name of God? I wish, writes Francis Jeanson, "to exist, not for God, but for those who are my brothers," my fellowmen. "And in order not to run the risk of betraying that duty of solidarity. . . , I will discard . . . every other justice and every other love . . . , and I will endeavor to the best of my ability to establish them even better in this life here on earth. . . . If God exists, I believe that he will find in that attitude what is due to him."[40]

Only the spectacle of the betrayal of authentic Christianity by those who called themselves Christians can have driven him to such a view. But it is this kind of "atheism" that purifies the air and re-awakens sincere Christians to their "divine" duty to establish justice and love on earth. Realizing that their own concrete actions and policies do not carry a divine guarantee,

40. Francis Jeanson, "Athéisme et liberté," *Lumière et Vie,* vol. 13 (1954), p. 96.

they will join their fellowmen in the search for truth and the establishment of values which remain the never-ended task of man's self-realization as the image and likeness of God.

SUGGESTED READINGS

Sartre, *Being and Nothingness*, tr. by Hazel E. Barnes, Philosophical Library, New York, 1956.

Existentialism and Humanism, Methuen, London, 1948.

The Devil and the Good Lord, Knopf, New York, 1960.

Merleau-Ponty, *In Praise of Philosophy*, Northwestern University Press, 1963.

Phenomenology of Perception, Humanities Press, New York, 1962.

Sense and Nonsense, Northwestern University Press, 1964; especially "Concerning Marxism" and "Faith and Good Faith."

Signs, Northwestern University Press, 1964; especially "Man and Adversity."

Luijpen, *Phenomenology and Atheism*, Ch. VI.

Existential Phenomenology, rev. ed., Duquesne University Press, 1969, Ch. IV (hatred and love).

CHAPTER SIX

PHILOSOPHY AND THE EXISTENCE OF GOD

1. INTRODUCTION

IN THE PRECEDING CHAPTERS we have unmasked the hidden atheism often present in the believers' affirmation of God. We saw how making God a physical factor explaining the phenomena of nature is a denial of the only true sense in which one can speak of God and that, for man who has come of age with respect to nature, all gods of thunder and lightning and other physical phenomena are simply idols to be discarded.

Similarly, we saw that atheism is an ingredient of any belief which makes God sanction the social privileges of the few and keep the poor and oppressed in their appointed stations of servitude. We rejected the god who guarantees the morality of the "establishment" by acting as its celestial policeman, the god who is an "unstared stare" and prevents man from being the creator of a world of meaning, the god whom theologians can dial when they are in doubt. The god who is the supreme craftsman, the super-economist, the super-physician, the super-psychiatrist and the super-farmer is gone forever. The only God who can still make sense to modern man is a God who transcends this world altogether, who is not a substitute for man's ignorance of the world, not a crutch to lean on for the fulfillment of his worldly needs.

At the same time, we saw in the preceding chapters that very often the atheist's rejection of God was a reaction to a faulty conception of God by those who believe in him. Generally speaking, these atheists rejected a god who prevents man from being himself as a pursuer of science, a social being, a cultural being, a moral being. And it was pointed out that the "true" concept of God also demands the elimination of all such objectionable features. But we have not as yet raised the all-important question, Does God exist? This question must now be faced.

Anyone who expects philosophy to come up with a proof for God's existence that will convince everyone or at least demonstrably expose the bad faith of unbelievers will be sadly disappointed. Besides, he misunderstands the possibilities open to philosophy. Not even in the "Age of Faith," the Middle Ages, did philosophers consider themselves entitled to offer such a proof. Thomas Aquinas' celebrated "five ways" (*S.T.*, I, q.2, a.3) do not end with the words: "And in this way God's existence is proved," but with the formula: "And this is what people mean when they speak of God" or other words to the same effect. He thereby indicates that the philosophical consideration throws a certain light on the question of what people mean by God, but cannot by itself make man say: "God exists."

2. CALLING THE NAME "GOD"

What does the religious man, the believer in God, mean when he calls the name "God"? This question may and indeed must be raised because, as a matter of fact, there are believers, just as also, as a matter of fact, there are artists. One might perhaps be inclined to think that there ought not to be any artists, but there are; similarly, one might be inclined to think that there ought not to be any believers, but there are. And if there are artists and believers, one can and must ask what they want. What does the artist want when he creates a work of art? What does the believer want when he calls the name "God"?

Let us first note that the believer, as a matter of fact, wants to *call* God's name. He does not merely intend to "establish" and "describe" that "God is" or that "God is this or that." What he does is a *calling* of God's name, a *shouting*, a *whispering* of his name; it is a praying and singing, a cheering and wailing, a sorrowing and cursing: God!, Thank God!, Praise God!, God Allmighty!, Goddamn! The religious man does not "establish and describe" anything "about" God when he calls the name "God," but *he expresses his own existence.* He discerns a mystery, a "depth" in his own existence whose message he cannot express in objectifying terms of being together with others in the world. A child is born and the religious man exclaims, "God!" He is healthy or sick and he exclaims, "God!" He sexually unites with a fellowman and in his ecstasy he cries out, "God!" He is dying and he shouts, "God!" At the rising and the setting of the sun, in the pale light of the moon and the stars, at the roaring of the sea, the undulation of the wheat, the threatening of the sky, the bubbling of a spring and the germinating of the seed, he exclaims, "God!" When he is victorious in battle and when he is defeated, when he lives in poverty and when he prospers, when he suffers injustice and when he is vindicated, the religious man cries out, "God!" He calls, he shouts, he whispers, "God!" He prays, he sings, he cheers, he laments, he sorrows and he curses the name "God!"

From the time when man explicitly began to reflect upon himself he has also attempted to speak about the mystery, the "depth" in his existence, to which he gave expression by the name "God." Some people managed to do this in a highly gifted way; there are not only scientific and ethical but also religious geniuses. What they said made it possible for others to "see" the mystery in their own existence. And it is the "seeing" of this mystery that makes man exclaim, "God!"

Once again, full emphasis must be put on the term "exclaim," for the mystery in human existence is misjudged when man's calling-out is *replaced* by a purely "stating description" in which "God" becomes the subject of a judgment. The calling of God's name cannot be *replaced* by statements such as:

God gives us a child;
God makes me healthy;
God sends me an illness;
God has connected intense pleasure with the sexual act;
God makes the sun rise and set, and he has put the moon and the stars in the firmament;
God makes the sea roar, the grain undulate, the storm erupt, the spring well up and the seed germinate;
God gives us victory in battle;
God inflicts a defeat on us;
God sends me poverty;
God gives me wealth;
God punishes evil;
God rewards the good;
God intervenes in history;
God rewards me;
God punishes me;
God leads us out of Egypt.

The calling of God's name, we said, cannot be *replaced* by a flat descriptive statement in which the name "God" becomes the subject of a judgment, as is the case in the preceding list of examples. Everyone, however, knows that the religious man, no matter in which phase of history he lived or lives, makes this kind of statement. He does express himself in the way we have said it can *not* be done.

This is not all, however. Not only does the religious man express himself in the way we said it can *not* be done; he is, moreover, entirely insensitive to anything that can be brought to bear against his statements. He truly is like one of the two explorers spoken of in Anthony Flew's parable.[1] Discovering a beautiful bed of flowers in the midst of a forest, this explorer says: "A gardener must have been at work here." His companion doubts it but is willing to verify his statement; the presence of that gardener somehow must be subject to verification. But even when they surround the bed of flowers with an electric fence and guard it with watch-dogs, there is no sign of a gardener. The "believing" explorer, however, is not at all discouraged. He simply asserts that the gardener is an invisible gardener and, therefore, cannot be perceived; he is odorless, so that the dogs cannot smell him; and he is without a body, so that the electric fence cannot affect him.

The religious man is indeed like such an explorer. He seems to remain unaffected by what the pursuers of science tell him about the reproduction of children, about health, sickness and death, about fertility and carnal pleasure. He knows that astrophysics tells us many things about the sun, the moon and the stars, and he knows that the meteorologist predicts the stormy roaring of the sea, the thunderstorm and the shining of the sun. He is not unacquainted with the fact that strategists explain military victories and defeats, and that economists can predict poverty and prosperity. The religious man does not deny what the pursuers of science tell him, but it does not seem to affect his religiousness. What does this mean?

It means that he goes past the *flat, descriptive* and *explanatory* statements in which the sciences speak of being bodily in the world together with others because, implicitly or explicitly, he "knows" that his own "statements about God" do not have a purely stating, descriptive and explanatory meaning—no more than a young man's statement about his girl, "She is a

---

1. "Theology and Falsification," *New Essays in Philosophical Theology*, ed. by Anthony Flew and Alasdair MacIntyre, SCM Press, London, 9th ed., 1969, pp. 96-99.

peach," should be understood as a botanical statement. Although the religious man uses sentences which have the external form of stating, describing and explaining something about God, they *intend* to express the "depth" in human existence, they *intend* to put into words being-man as orientation-to, they *intend* to touch the mystery contained in a subjectivity immersed in a body and involved in the world. Implicitly or explicitly, the religious man "knows" that this mystery is not accessible to the sciences because they do not speak of man as existence but as an "ingredient" or object of the sciences. And scientific "ingredients" are not religious.

The "Self" of Self-Understanding

If the calling of the name "God" is explicitated as a mode of man's self-understanding, i.e., if a statement about God is called a statement about man, it can easily happen that one will conclude from this that *therefore* God is "really nothing," "Nothing in objective reality," but at most "something in subjectivity."

It is striking that the representatives of this standpoint start from the assumption that "something" only is "something" if it is either "something objective" or "something subjective." But this very presupposition dooms to failure their dialogue with those who claim that a statement about God is a statement about man, for the latter precisely refuse to start with that presupposition. Their model is not the separation of the subjective and the objective but the "unity of their reciprocal implication."

If the "self" of "self-understanding" is conceived as an isolated "self," one who accepts the statement, "Speaking of God is speaking of man," could indeed be accused of subjectivism. But today those who, following Bultmann and Heidegger, make this assertion certainly do not conceive the "self," man's subjectivity, as an isolated "self." Self-understanding is the understanding of an *existent* subject, in other words, of a subject who is himself only in unity with what is not the subject, viz., the body, the world, the other. If, then, the physicist speaks of the world of physics, his speaking is at the same time a speaking of himself because the "speaker" is the unity of the reciprocal implication of subjectivity "and" world. Accordingly, the statement that speaking about the world is speaking about man should not be interpreted as if it implied that speaking about the world says "really nothing" about the world but only something about subjective contents. For subject "and" world constitute a unity of reciprocal implication.

We do not wish to suggest that the statement, "Speaking about God is speaking about man," is now clear. The only thing we have shown so far is that one cannot conclude that God is "really nothing," "nothing objectively" but at most "something in the subject." If we were to assert that God is "something objective," we would not be speaking about the God of Christianity. Fertility and sexual pleasure, health and sickness, the sun, the moon and the stars, thunderstorms and springs, victories and defeats, poverty and prosperity, justice and injustice are "something objective." There are religions which worship these beings as God. But the God of Christianity is *not* a being; God *is* not.

When we say that God *is* not, we re-affirm that the God of Christianity cannot be put on a par with anything that is not-God. The religious man calls the name "God" to express the "depth" in his existence, a "depth" which cannot be expressed in the objectifying terms of being bodily together with others in the world. Although this cannot be done, the religious man does it anyhow; he makes use of sentences which have the external form of stating, describing and explaining sentences. He makes God the subject of such sentences and borrows predicates for him from man's being bodily together with others in the world. But even in these sentences he *intends* to speak about the "depth" in his self-understanding as a being bodily together with others in the world. That's why Bultmann and Ogden can say that speaking about God is speaking about man. But a Christian who speaks about God and makes God the subject of a judgment doesn't intend to say that God *is*. He will *deny* the "thousand qualifications" of God as soon as he has affirmed them. Flew wonders what has to happen before one would be willing to admit that God does not love us. Our answer would be that nothing whatsoever has to happen for this and that we feel obliged to add those words as soon as we say, "God loves us."

3. METAPHYSICS

Let us return to the objection that God is "really nothing," "nothing objective" but at most "something subjective." If we retain its terminology, unacceptable as it is, we would have to say that all endeavors to show that God "is" "something objective" must be viewed as attempts to disclose the "depth" in human existence. Such an attempt is a "proof" for God's existence, the key-stone of "metaphysics." There is need to think metaphysically "about" God because man's calling of God's name can degenerate. It can lead to the sacrifice of little children, the burning of widows and temple prostitution; it can function as an opiate, it can induce people to antagonize the sciences and to preserve unjust political, social and economic systems; it can lead to obscurantism, ignorance, poverty, illness, neglect of duty, intolerance, tyranny and psychical aberrations.

With the atheists, we have rejected all such things. But we did not feel obliged to become adherents of atheism because we conceive the "depth" in human existence as man's orientation to the *transcendent* God. It is the task of metaphysics, of the "proof" for God's existence, to disclose this orientation. Before attempting to do this, let us first present a brief survey of metaphysics with respect to our question.

There are thinkers who claim that all metaphysical statements must be rejected as meaningless. This is the position taken by A. J. Ayer and many analytic philosophers. They claim that to affirm, deny or even profess agnosticism with respect to God are equally meaningless positions *because* they are metaphysical.

Metaphysical statements are meaningless, says Ayer, because they refer to something suprasensual and therefore cannot be verified in the way he understands this term. Ayer holds that only tautological and empirical statements are meaningful. In a tautological statement, however, the predicate adds nothing to the subject, so that one cannot get anywhere with this kind of statement; it does not express any reality. Empirical statements, on the other hand, are based on the observation of reality. But the statement, "God exists," is not the affirmation of something observable in reality but refers to something transcending reality. This makes it at once unverifiable; therefore, it is neither true nor false but simply meaningless. The same applies of course also to the statement, "God does not exist." Even agnosticism is meaningless. For the agnostic says: "Either God exists or he does not exist, but I am unable to determine which of these two propositions is true." In other words, he fails to see that both positions are equally beyond verification and therefore meaningless nonsense.[2]

Ayer's standpoint is much too simplistic. The very way he conceives "verification" eliminates even the *question* raised by the metaphysician. The metaphysician also wants to "verify," but the question is whether verification can always be made in the way Ayer proposes. One who assumes that *only* statements like, "A cat is sitting on the mat," are verifiable will inevitably

2. A. Ayer, *Language, Truth and Logic*, Dover, New York, n.d., pp.. 114 ff.

come to the "conclusion" that metaphysical statements are meaningless. But there is no genuine conclusion here; everything has already been settled beforehand through the tacit presupposition.

Others reject the "metaphysical affirmation" of God because they take it to refer to God *in himself*. When Descartes had isolated the mind from the body, the world and God, the only way he could safeguard their reality was by saying that they were something more than a mere idea in the mind, by ascribing to them some being-in-themselves. That's why the body, the world and God became for him the body-in-itself, the world-in-itself, God-in-himself. A similar split had also occurred previously in scholastic philosophy: every essence, including that of man, was necessarily and immutably true in itself as it had been created by God. And God also was a God-in-himself. But once God is posited as a God-in-himself, divorced from man, then, in principle, man has no relationship whatsoever to him; he is not a God-for-man. That's why Gabriel Marcel could exclaim that traditional "theodicy is atheism." He rejects such an inhuman God-in-himself but only in order to "affirm" the authentic God-for-man. What should be kept in mind here is that man is the original sayer of "is" and that any attempt to eliminate man as the one who "affirms" that something "is" in order to assert this something-in-itself tries the impossible. If I eliminate the subject who says "is," there is no possibility whatsoever to maintain the "is" of that which is affirmed. "Is" always means "is-for-me" or "is-for-us," never "is-in-itself."

Still others reject the "metaphysical affirmation" of God because they find this affirmation embodied in an idealistic or scientistic system. In a scientistic system the "affirmation" of

God as cause simply represents God as the first in the series of causes considered in the sciences. God is then reduced to a worldly cause; he is no longer transcendent in the true sense of the term. The denial of such a god is, as we saw, a good kind of atheism. Idealistic systems, on the other hand, tend to identify the relatively "little" subject who man is with the Absolute Subject or God. The latter is supposed to act in and through the little subject. What really happens then, of course, is that the little subject claims to speak and act with the authority of God, ascribing a divine guarantee to his words and deeds. Obviously, this kind of "affirmation" of God is rightly rejected.

Finally, there are thinkers who do not consider it necessary to reject the "metaphysical affirmation" of God in order to safeguard an authentic "affirmation" of God. They view all objectivistic, scientistic and idealistic interpretations of metaphysics as degenerations of man's authentic metaphysical dimension. In their eyes, metaphysics is always "anthropological," that is, it says something about being-for-man; and they view the possibility of metaphysically "affirming" God solely as a possibility of "affirming" the existence of a transcendent God-for-man.

From this standpoint the "affirmation" of God simply expresses that man is a being-for-the-other-than-himself and that this being-for-the-other possesses a depth which transcends the world and fellowmen and is orientated to the supraworldly reality called "God." Let us now see one of the ways in which man can give expression to this depth dimension of his being. We will take our starting point for it in the traditional inspiration of metaphysics without, however, committing any of the above-mentioned mistakes. This inspiration lies in so-called "contingency," but understood in the metaphysical sense and not in the strictly anthropological sense of Merleau-Ponty.

4. CONTINGENCY

If we ask the question, Why is there something rather than nothing?, then anyone who realizes that man is the original "sayer" of "is" must answer: because man is. Man is the one who through his consciousness makes everything be-for-him, and this being-for-him is the only way one can speak about being.

But this is merely a first answer to our question. It implies that in and by the "saying" of "is" which man's existence itself is the beings "come about" *as* beings. Existence is the primordial "affirmation" of the beings precisely as beings, as opposed to nothing. The question, Why is there something rather than nothing?, is not interested in the particular "why" of things, animals, men, mountains, eggs and cloud layers; it is concerned with what is common in those different beings, viz., the fact that they are beings.

This concern reaches its proper level at the moment when one realizes that beings as beings are not by virtue of their own essence. If they were, they would be *pure* "to be"; nature or essence and "to be" would be identical in them. The very fact that there are *many* beings implies that they cannot be pure "to be." To be many means to be different since the absence of any difference whatsoever means total identity or oneness. Now, to be different can only mean that one being has something which the other does not have; otherwise the two would be identical and, consequently, not many but one. All this means that the "to be" of the beings of my metaphysical experience implies a certain "not to be"; in other words, they are not pure "to be" but merely *have* "to be," they only share in it.

On the other hand, there is no escape from the fact that the beings of my experience *are*. Now, if they are not by virtue of their own essence, then they must be by virtue of *something else*. This is what is meant by the metaphysical sense of the term "contingent": it refers to beings which *are*, but not of themselves but by virtue of something else.

To be by virtue of something else is the same as being by the influence of something else; it means being-caused. Beings, then, that reveal themselves as contingent reveal that they are caused beings. Being-contingent is the same as being-caused.

When this stage is reached, we must be very careful in asking what causes contingent beings to be. Inquiring about their cause is not like asking, Why are there lice in the vineyard? One who asks about the cause of an agricultural pest assumes an attitude of questioning which co-determines the kind of answer that can be meaningful from his standpoint. Whatever the answer is, it applies only to the particular realm circumscribed by his agricultural question, to a particular region of being.

The metaphysician, however, cannot be satisfied with an answer referring to a particular region of being and the kind of causality that is appropriate to it. The agriculturalist who explains why the lice are still in the vineyard merely explains why they overcame the pesticide. He does not explain why they "overcame" non-being. Such a question is meaningless to him as an agriculturalist. Only the metaphysician can ask the question why contingent beings are in spite of their contingency.

What, then, can be the cause why contingent beings *are*? This cause certainly cannot be any being belonging to the universe of contingent beings, for each one of them itself also is contingent. Now, this means that the whole universe has no sufficient reason for its being in itself.

If only one could say that nothing is! Then all difficulties would vanish, for "nothing is much more simple" than being. But there is not nothing, for being *is*. Therefore, the other-than-being . . . . .Why the dots? Why don't we say: "The other-than-being *is*"? Because one who without any further ado says that the other-than-being *is*, has already made this other-than-being a contingent being, a being of which one can say "without any further ado" that it *is*. By leaving the dots, we indicate that there is indeed a "depth" in human existence as the original affirmation of being. This original affirmation *is* the transcendence of the affirmation of being. When he experiences this original transcendence of being, the religious man exclaims "God."

Retrospect. It should be clear now why above we had to say that *calling* the name "God" cannot be replaced by a judgment in which God occurs as a subject to whom a predicate is ascribed. For otherwise we would say that God *is*, and this is blasphemous.

Nevertheless, we said, the religious man often expresses himself in that way which we consider unjustifiable. Let us add that there is no objection to this *provided* he does *not* conceive his statements as flat descriptive statements. If he conceives them in this way, he fails to understand himself and sooner or later his statements will be replaced by others. Let us explain this. The religious man says:

God gives me a child;
God has connected intense pleasure with the sexual act;
God gives us victory in battle;
God sends me an illness;
God gives us wealth and poverty.

If these statements are conceived as flat descriptive statements, their origin and original intention are misjudged and then they are quickly replaced by other statements such as:

The gynecologist gives me a child;
A nervous stimulation causes the pleasure of the sexual act;
Eisenhower gives us victory in battle;
A virus is the cause of my illness;
The Treasury gives us wealth and poverty.

"God is Dead." These considerations can be applied in a simple way to an actual topic. Some people say: "God is dead." If this statement is conceived as a purely "descriptive," "stating" and "judging" sentence, "God" must be conceived as a being. The sentence then does not have a meaning which fundamentally differs from the statement: "Jim is dead." That Jim is dead means that Jim once was but that now there is no Jim. That God is dead means, according to Hamilton and Altizer, "that there once was a God—but that now there is no God."[3] In other words, Hamilton and Altizer present God as "a Jim" of whom one can express in predicates what he *is*; he is presented as a being. But Hamilton and Altizer don't realize that they are doing this. The same must be said of Christians who oppose Hamilton and Altizer and understand the statement, "God is alive," as a purely "stating," "descriptive" and "judging" sentence. They, too, present God as a being, as one does in the sentence: "My mother-in-law is alive."

5. UNSATISFACTORY CHARACTER OF THE "PROOF"

Even when all the pitfalls mentioned at the beginning of this chapter are avoided, and even when the "proof" for God's existence is really understood, it displeases and disappoints both believers and unbelievers. For the unbeliever the "proof" goes too far; it points in a direction in which he does not want to go. For the believer it does not go far enough; he seeks a God to whom he can pray, whom he can love, for whom he can make music and dance and whom, on occasion, he can even curse. In other words, the religious man does not feel that he is exis-

3. *Radical Theology and the Death of God*, New York, 1966, Preface, p. X.

tentially involved through such a "proof." That's why he thinks that he can do without it. This is Marcel's objection to the "proof" for God's existence.

It must be granted at once that for a sincere believer God means much more than transcendent "to be" or the uncaused cause of contingent beings. If I ask a biologist to tell me what "my mother" means and he explains that it means that I was conceived in her womb and developed there, he answers my question in purely biological terms. But if I love my mother, she means much more to me than a purely biological progenitor; his answer leaves me dissatisfied. Yet, what he told me was true; I was conceived in her womb and developed there. If this had not happened, she would not have been my mother. I should not blame him for not saying more than he did, for as a biologist he was *unable* to say more.

Now, if my belief in God is to be an authentically human belief, a belief to which I as a being endowed with reason can subscribe, then this belief must have a rational justification; I must be intellectually convinced that God exists. The above-mentioned "proof" gives expression to this conviction: it makes it impossible for me to deify myself or any other worldly reality because none of them are a sufficient reason for their own existence. In this way the "proof" eliminates the danger that I'll raise any worldly reality to the rank of God or reduce God to a worldly reality.

Using again the above-mentioned comparison of "my mother," the biological process to which the scientist points cannot express what "my mother" means to me. But this process belongs to the integral reality which makes my mother be "my mother." It is even conceivable that in the case of a mix-up in a hospital nursery only a biologist would be able to determine who really is "my mother." Man may need the metaphysical "proof" of God's existence to determine who really is "his God" and who is nothing but a pseudo-god. From this standpoint, disappointing as the "proof" may be to the believer, it is not entirely useless nor meaningless.

The same objection can also be approached in a different way by paying attention to the various "language games" spoken of by modern linguistic analysis. The language game of faith in God is a language of proclamation, confession and orientation: the believer calls upon God, he shouts or whispers his name; he sings, praises, hails and curses his name. This kind of language does not intend to describe and explain anything about God, but voices what the religious man experiences in himself when he calls upon God. The language game of the believer is not the language game of description. Let us add another example to show this.

If during the night I suddenly hear a shout from my neighbor's house, "Fire! Fire!," I know that these words are not meant to describe and explain an objective condition existing in his dwelling. What he intends with his words is an appeal to me: "Come and help us." In a similar way, the language of faith is not descriptive but appealing, it does not merely state that something is but confesses, invites and orientates. The religious words, "God is with us," are not like the words, "There is a fly on the ceiling."

Now, the language of metaphysics is not a call but intends to describe what is. Thus the question that arises at once is whether the philosopher can ever *confess* God. There are, of course, many philosophers who are also sincere believers and therefore also confess God, but this is not the point. The question is whether the philosopher *as philosopher* can confess God. Before answering it, let us first make a comparison. Can a physicist *as* a physicist speak about beauty, can a biologist *as* a biologist speak about the ethics of germ warfare? Obviously not;

within the perspective of physical science beauty never appears, and from the standpoint of biology ethical considerations are one hundred per cent irrelevant. Aesthetics is not a branch of physics, and ethics is not a biological discipline. But the human beings who pursue physical science and biology can speak about beauty and ethics; and as human beings they have every right—and duty—to take aesthetic and ethical dimensions into consideration. In a similar way, then, people who are philosophers have a right to confess God; when they do this, however, they no longer act as philosophers but as believers.

By virtue of its own intention, in the name of its own attitude of asking questions, philosophy cannot confess God. The philosopher as philosopher pursues a critical function; he explores what is tenable in any statement whatsoever, including the confessing, calling and orientating statements of the believer. *As* a philosopher, he cannot go beyond this. Philosophy demands of him that he be "reserved" with respect to all calls and proclamations. Even if his critical investigation of a religious call terminates in a positive "report," he cannot do more than offer a purely *descriptive* affirmation of what the call contains. His situation is like that of a man who hears the cry, "Fire!," opens the window, checks for signs of smoke and flames and then says: "Yes, there is a fire." As long as he does this, he merely *describes* whether there is substance to the cry; he doesn't answer it. But if my checking whether there is substance to the cry shows that indeed there is a fire, then this cry appears to me also in a different perspective; it becomes an appeal for help which I ought to accept.

One could argue that if philosophy as such cannot listen to the language of calls and proclamations, if it can never arrive at confessing, then philosophy is of no use with respect to man's belief in God and his speaking about God. This doesn't follow, however. Let us illustrate the matter by an example from another field of "calls" and "invitations." After a long, tiring drive with friends through a thinly settled part of the country, we come to a crossroad with a small rural inn. A sign proclaims: JOE'S FRIENDLY EATING PLACE, and underneath in smaller letters: *dinner is ready to serve.* The sentence, "Dinner is ready to serve," is not purely the description of a fact but a call and an invitation to eat. If one has no intention of inviting others to "come and get it," one doesn't play the "language game" of a call and abstains from hanging up such a sign.

On the other hand, if we enter the "friendly eating place" and find that the dinner is not ready to serve and that the kitchen stove is not even on, Joe cannot excuse himself by saying that the language of his sign is merely a call and an invitation and that it does not intend to describe the objective situation. If his sign is not based on an objective situation, then, we angrily point out to him, he should show greater reserve and cease seducing unwary travellers to stop for nothing.

Anyone who knows the tricks innkeepers use to lure customers also knows that not every sign is a reliable call and invitation to stop for dinner. Is it meaningless, then, if my friends ask me first to check whether the dinner is actually ready to serve before they make a decision? So I enter and submit the language of the sign to verification. I discover that in this case the dinner is as a matter of fact ready and, returning to my friends in the car, I communicate to them the result of my critical investigation: "Yes, the dinner is ready." All I can do is use descriptive language; I state that the situation ("the dinner is ready") which is presupposed by the call does actually exist. My description is not an invitation, but it is very meaningful for anyone who wishes to consider the invitation itself.

The role of philosophy with respect to the religious call is similar to that of the man who checks whether dinner is really ready to serve. All the philosopher as philosopher can do is verify—in his own philosophical way—the claim and then communicate the result of his verification in descriptive language. All he can do is warn people not to "rush in for dinner" when he finds that nothing is ready. And when he finds that dinner is ready, he can merely present this fact as a fact to us; it is up to us to accept the invitation or drive on. Considering the large number of false claims—we have seen some of them in the preceding chapters—the philosopher's checking is not entirely superfluous. At the same time, his reserve in limiting himself to "checking" is as uninspiring to believers in God as is a father's scrutiny of his prospective son-in-law's ability to support a family is to the impatient daughter in love.

But one cannot disregard the tedious task of the philosopher in this matter simply because it is uninspiring. For disregarding the philosopher's function to check the credibility of all "calls" means disregarding that man can act authentically only if he acts also rationally. But once the philosopher as philosopher has checked the credentials of a religious call and found it to be authentic, then this call addresses itself also to him as a human being having a religious dimension. Then he also must decide whether to accept the call or reject it. And if he accepts, then he confesses God.

The "Empirical Spirit of Our Age"

For Van Buren the attempt to express the "depth" in human existence is in principle meaningless. The principle leading him to this view is rather simple. It is "the empirical spirit of the age." To whatever "left-wing" theologians of existence say he adds the question, Do you really think that this means anything at all to the empirical-minded man of our time? He asks them where they find their "modern man," for their "modern man" does not appear to be the scientist whom Van Buren has all the time in mind. He is *a priori* convinced that this "disregard" of the scientist is intolerable. For Bultmann to speak about man is equiprimordially to speak about God because speaking about man *cannot* be exhausted by making him an "ingredient" of the sciences. When Bultmann tries to speak of the "proper reality of man," Van Buren is thinking of man as an "ingredient" of the sciences and asking himself what the name "God" can possibly still mean here.[4] Once this presupposition is granted, his question is, of course, very legitimate, but the crucial point is whether his presupposition itself is legitimate.

The answer would seem to be in the negative. The sciences do not speak about the essence of man as "existence"; now, it is precisely as "existent" that man is religious or not religious.

That's why we would prefer to be more reserved than Ogden, who says that the demand to demythologize which necessarily arises from modern man's situation, must be accepted *without qualification.*[5] The words "without qualification" evoke objections. The reason is this. The situation of modern man includes the absolutism of the scientific and technological attitude. Now, one who sees the limitation of this absolutism simply cannot make the situation of modern man without qualification the norm of what is relevant or irrelevant with respect to man. It is relevant that a young man calls his girl a "peach." If modern man no longer understands this and demands that he use only the psycho-diagnostic models which were created when he and his girl became "ingredients" of science, then modern man is lost and that young lover will never be able to say again what he wanted to say.

Conclusion

If statements about God, despite their outward appearance, do not have a purely stating, descriptive and explanatory meaning, the question must be asked whether, after all, the best language of which the religious man can make use is not mythical language. But even if one doubts this, it still remains true that Bultmann's program of demythologization may not be absolut-

4. *The Secular Meaning of the Gospel*, London, 1963, pp. 68 ff.
5. S. Ogden, *Christ without Myth*, London, 1962, p. 148.

ized and understood as a demand to eliminate all myths from our speaking about God. Bultmann himself never demanded or intended this; he solely objected to false interpretations of the myths, in particular, those interpretations which conceive myths as scientific or historical explanations.

Gusdorf offers us an extensive discussion of the possibility of giving mythical language again a place in our speaking about God. A pre-condition of this possibility is that we abandon rationalism and scientism. For absolutized reason all situations in which man calls the name "God" have no other meaning than that of a logical operation. But the primacy of logic over existence deprives the latter of all depth. The same applies to scientism. As soon as man is reduced to an "ingredient" of the sciences, all "depth" is at once removed from his existence. The use of mythical stories to speak about God presupposes the rehabilitation of what Husserl calls the "life world." It is in this "life world" that the "depth" in human existence in which man calls the name "God" becomes visible.[6]

Myths, however, also can run amuck. They can push man along on a road without exit or leading to his destruction. They can suggest a "depth" that does not exist and demand a surrender that cannot be justified. That's why the mythical consciousness also must be placed under the control of a critical authority. And this critical authority is metaphysics.

SUGGESTED READINGS

A. Ayer, *Language, Truth and Logic*, Dover, New York, n.d.
John A. Robinson, *Honest to God*, London, 1963.

Martin Heidegger, *Essays in Metaphysics*, New York, 1960.

6. G. Gusdorf, *Mythe et Metaphysique*, Paris, 1964, pp. 181 ff.

Religion and Atheism

Thomas J. Altizer and William Hamilton, *Radical Theology and the Death of God*, New York, 1966.

Paul Van Buren, *The Secular Meaning of the Gospel*, London, 1963.

Schubert M. Ogden, *Christ without Myth*, London, 1962.

Ian T. Ramsey, *Religious Language*, London, 1957.

Christian Discourse, London, 1965.

INDEX OF NAMES

INDEX OF SUBJECT MATTER

Index of Subject Matter